Gaido's
FAMOUS SEAFOOD RESTAURANT

Gaido's

FAMOUS SEAFOOD RESTAURANT

A COOKBOOK CELEBRATING 100 YEARS

Published by Gaido Chefs Two, Inc.
Copyright © 2011 by
Gaido Chefs Two, Inc.
3802 Seawall Boulevard
Galveston, Texas 77550
409-762-9625
www.gaidos.com

Photography © by Kenny Haner
www.kennyhaner.com

Caught in Galveston Bay
Served at GAIDO'S Famous SEAFOOD RESTAURANT

Library of Congress Control Number: 2010931413
ISBN: 978-0-615-34885-8

Edited, Designed, and Produced by
Favorite Recipes® Press
An imprint of
FRP.INC
A wholly owned subsidiary of Southwestern/
Great American, Inc.
P.O. Box 305142
Nashville, Tennessee 37230
800-358-0560

Art Director and Book Design: Starletta Polster
Editorial Director: Mary Cummings
Project Editor: Tanis Westbrook
Recipe Editor: Nicki Pendleton Wood, CCP

Manufactured in the United States of America
First Printing: 2011   20,000 copies

To order additional copies of our cookbook and
to order our homemade products, please visit
our Web site at www.gaidos.com.

Gaido's
FAMOUS SEAFOOD RESTAURANT

A *Cookbook* CELEBRATING 100 YEARS

Acknowledgments

These women worked tirelessly for three months testing and preparing the Gaido's recipes in their home kitchens. This was no easy task because most of the recipes had to be reduced from serving five hundred to serving eight to ten. Because of them, we know that these dishes can be made by home "chefs" as well as culinary chefs. We could not have created this cookbook without them, and it is impossible to thank these volunteers enough for their work and their input.

From left to right: Jan Parks, Donna Gartner, Jeanine Levin, Ellen Druss, Camille Tackaberry, Mary Kay Gaido, Sue Laabs, Barbara Visser, Cathy Geisinger, Lisa Schulte, Donna James (not pictured – Linda Goodman, Kathie Curry, Nancy O'Dowd)

Preface

One hundred years ago an Italian immigrant from Cercenasco, Italy, opened a café on Galveston Island. A keen businessman, San Giacinto Gaido established a loyal customer base by holding to his proprietor's motto, "learn what is wanted and then serve." This motto, carried on by the family's fourth generation, is still at the heart of a restaurant that has outlasted the fads, trends, and social pendulums of the last century.

The largest fresh fish house on the Gulf Coast, capable of serving 2,500 people in a day, continues to provide those who walk through its doors with fresh Gulf seafood.

To celebrate its centennial birthday, Gaido's Famous Seafood Restaurant has gathered all of the recipes that epitomize its Gulf Coast cuisine. With this cookbook, Gaido's hopes to share the great food and fond memories with its customers as well as pay tribute to those who have made the last century possible.

San Giacinto Gaido and
wife Josephine

Mike, S.J., and Fritz Gaido
on the Seawall

Welcoming guests upon their arrival, these vintage diving helmets have stood at Gaido's entrance for more than two decades. Donated by Mary Kay Gaido and added to the many historical collections found in the dining rooms, these relics have been quick to become the center of many photo ops.

Contents

Introduction

By 3 p.m. on a Friday afternoon in one of Texas's hot summer months, a steady flow of diners begin to spill into the lobby of Gaido's Restaurant. Perched atop the seawall in Galveston, Texas, facing the Gulf of Mexico, these visitors are welcomed with genuine southern warmth and hospitality accompanied by Texas humility and charm. While an unusual dinner hour for most, this is the norm for an out-of-the-ordinary restaurant. Hungry patrons remain undaunted by the wait, knowing a hundred years of classic fare await them when they take their seats.

PROPRIETOR'S MOTTO

"learn what is wanted and then serve"

"If you are not proud of it, don't serve it."

The long lines that brace the facade of the establishment did not form overnight, nor did they come about by chance. Rather, they were gradually built over the years by hard work, service based on simple values, and cuisine steeped in tradition. The ability to satisfy customers on a consistent basis is the common element that characterizes the handful of American restaurants that have celebrated their one-hundredth anniversaries. While each has their own formula for achieving guest satisfaction, Gaido's accomplishes this by continuing to embrace fundamental principles, anchored in honesty, trust, and respect, set by its founder, San Giacinto Gaido. To this day these cornerstones have influenced every food and service decision. These have been passed down from generation to generation in mottos and slogans.

Our task is not to educate the guest to our tastes or our preferences but to discover his tastes and his preferences and to serve accordingly. If you are not proud of it, don't serve it. Always trust the guest's ability to recognize genuine food quality and his willingness to pay accordingly. Never forget the guest is always right, especially when he is wrong. The very best advertising is word of mouth, so put it on the plate. Guests will freely give us their trust but only so long as we prove worthy of it."

Left to right: James Peques, Eddie Morris, Paulie Gaido, Charles Brooks, Wade Watkins

While the traditional dishes found on a Gaido's menu would be considered far from artisanal by the James Beard Foundation, the intangible ideals that are needed to produce them mirror those of some of the most renowned nouvelle cuisine chefs. It is only in practicing Fernand Pont's refined simplicity or in keeping with the freshest of ingredients from Bocuse that such consistent quality makes its way into Gaido's dining room. The Gaido family has always been passionate about food but has never considered food as art; instead, the focus has always been on taste. Gaido's all consuming commitment to taste begins with taking full advantage of its own geography. Galveston's front doors open onto an unparalleled bounty of shrimp and fish, while Galveston Bay provides an abundance of oysters and crabs unrivaled around the world. It is these items for which Gaido's is known, and it is these items that Gaido's does best. Its location also provides the restaurant a close proximity to not only great seafood but a number of wonderful cultures and cuisines that have influenced the menu greatly. Throughout the years, chefs and family members have infused Gaido's menus with traditional southern deep frying, Southwest open-flame grilling, and Creole flavor.

This picture featuring Mr. Alfred Hitchcock and Mike Gaido is a favorite among employees, guests, and family. This is likely due to the fortuitous angle at which the picture was taken, showing what is considered one of the most famous silhouettes in the world.

Like its centenarian counterparts, Gaido's has welcomed its fair share of presidents and heads-of-state as well as athletes and entertainers. Many a business deal and promise of support for a political candidate has been made in one of the private dining rooms. Through the years, however, it is the everyday guests who chose to share a birthday, anniversary, or proposal at a table in a quiet corner that makes the Gaido family and its staff most proud.

GEORGE BUSH

Jan 31, '93

Dear Paul,
I just want to thank
you for the lovely dinner -
I loved being back at Gaido's.
So did Barbara. My respects
to your Mother, a true lady.
Sincerely, Gq Bush

Barbara Bush, Rick Gaido, George Bush, Michael Gaido

Refusing to yield to the temptation of ill-conceived expansion, the emphasis has never shifted from 39th and Seawall Boulevard.

This cookbook is dedicated to all of the guests who have honored Gaido's with their friendship and patronage through these years; only with their support was such tenure possible. This cookbook is intended not only as a compilation of recipes but also as a sharing of the experience and knowledge that comes from selecting, preparing, and serving Gulf Coast cuisine. It is made in the hope that the reader will use it as a reference and guide for cooking and entertaining with the same confidence and love that was shared by a family grateful and honored to be given a chance to serve them.

WAITER COINS

"Brass" coins used for waiter "banks" handled cash exchanged between waiters and Gaido's restaurant when it was located at Murdoch's bathhouse.

Circa 1916–1934

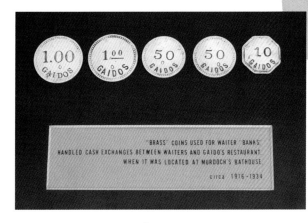

"BRASS" COINS USED FOR WAITER "BANKS" HANDLED CASH EXCHANGES BETWEEN WAITERS AND GAIDO'S RESTAURANT WHEN IT WAS LOCATED AT MURDOCH'S BATHHOUSE.

circa 1916–1934

April 28, 1940
11:30 P M
Houston, Texas

Hi Mike & Party: Sorry I havn't written sooner, because we have been pretty busy, everything is going along all right, and happy, I put $200.00 down on that land and will get the deed in a week or ten days, I talked to Dr.Thoma the other day and a few other friends we have, and why don't we put at least 2500.00 dollars down and pay the rest in 90 days, and save about 500.00 dollars in intrest in 5 years. or pay thirty or forty dollars in 90 days, because the money in the box is not doing us any good and it could be working for us and saveing us money. Than we could borrow all we want on the land we own.Than Mr Jaffet is willing to lend us money at 3 or 4 % on a new building ..

I talked to Mr. Finn and told him we bought the Land and he said find and he also said the new size is better than the first. and he said to let him know when we are ready..

Well here are the answers:::

Monday	260.55	we beat Sunday
Tuesday	144.61	Pretty good
Wednesday	132.79	Not so good
Thursday	270.59	Front and Back doors packed when you called..
Friday	242.99	Not Bad ,,,,
Saturday	311.00	Pretty good hu..
Sunday	250.00	Maybe ,, Rain all day and plenty hard..

Well Tell all hello and have a good time

Fritz.

Weyman said to tell all his women hello

Booked 3 more parties for upstairs...

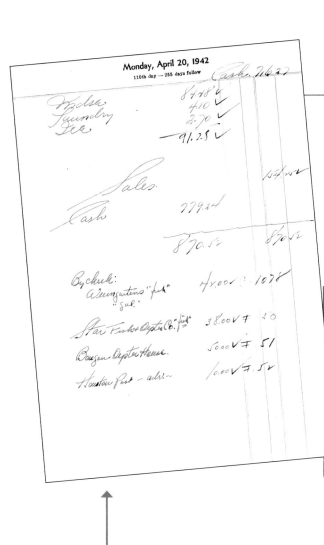

Monday, April 20, 1942
110th day — 255 days follow

MONEY LOG

A page taken from Gaido's money log for the year 1942 shows that on April 6, 1942, oysters were still in season. The log is also a reminder of the everyday acquisitions of such perishable products and the everyday purchase of ice.

1942   1947   1958   1967   2006

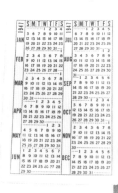

Family History

It is unlikely that San Giacinto Gaido had little if any memory of Cercenasco, Italy, where he was born in 1886. The youngest of six children born to Giuseppe and Antonina Grosso Gaido, Cinto was but two years old when his widowed mother brought him and his older siblings to join family in Galveston, Texas. After his mother died a short time later,

San Giacinto Gaido

Cinto resided in a local orphan's home. Not surprisingly, he never forgot that experience nor his "rescue" by older sister Katherine Colombo. Like so many immigrants of his time, especially the orphans, Cinto started working not long after he started school. His many jobs included a stint as a window washer for the Felman's Dry Goods store in downtown Galveston, but he found his true vocation when he joined the wait staff at several Galveston eateries. Determined to be in business for himself, he opened a sandwich shop in downtown Galveston and parlayed that success into opening Gaido's on the Seawall Boulevard in the brand new Murdoch's Bathhouse in 1911. Cinto's respect for and trust in his restaurant patrons along with a deep and abiding commitment to food quality and friendly, unpretentious service gave succeeding generations of Gaido's a solid blueprint for success. His legacy, however, would be so much more—by refusing the easy

money that would have come as an
accomplice to bootlegging. Cinto
made a conscious choice to preserve
the public's respect for the Gaido's as a
hardworking Italian family making an
honest living.

All three of Cinto's sons had
successful careers. His namesake
S.J. started a pipe coating business
in a then up-and-coming Houston;
while Fritz, ably assisted by his son

Rick, daughter Joann, and close
friend Waymon Staples, delighted
Houstonians with fresh Gulf seafood
served in the Gaido tradition on
South Main. It was his oldest son,
Mike, who chose to carry on the
Gaido's in Galveston, which was not
at all surprising given his life-long
love affair with his hometown.
Working closely with brother-in-law
and general manager Harry Rabe,
Mike built on the Gaido reputation.

Effie, S.J., Mike, Fritz, Kewpie, and Eunice Gaido

Mike Gaido

Top-quality seafood and first-class service ultimately made Gaido's of Galveston a must-stop for visitors to the island and a destination restaurant in its own right. In many ways Mike was an even better businessman than restaurateur, and may have been a still better architect had he chosen to follow that dream. He deftly coupled his remarkable insight into what the public desired in a seaside seafood restaurant with a penchant for expansion and remodeling.

It was Mike who was responsible for moving Gaido's sixteen blocks west of Murdoch's Bathhouse to its present location on 39th Street. This resulted in the opening of the adjacent Galveston Pelican Club and the café next door that ultimately became Casey Gaido's. He was a man of few words, but his sons remember well the restaurant business wisdom he imparted.

Gaido's Seafood Restaurant located in
Murdoch's Bath House 1920s

If your food is really good, guests will find you no matter where you are located and drive a long distance, often right past your competition, to dine with you. Tend to your own knitting. Don't worry about what others are doing; concentrate instead on what is going on inside your own doors. Guests like to see restaurateurs reinvest in their businesses, especially with new décor from time to time, but nothing trumps great food and friendly attentive service. You can't eat sheetrock! Don't be afraid to season your food; guests are searching for taste sensations when they dine out. Dress the part and always look your very best. You are not only selling fresh seafood, you are selling yourself. —Mike Gaido

Murdoch's Bath House 1920s

"you can never go wrong doing what is right"

Much like his own father, Mike's legacy to succeeding generations of Gaido's was more than a reputation for first-class seafood and warm hospitality. Mike insisted that "you can never go wrong doing what is right" and that those who found success in business had greater responsibilities than those who were only marginally successful. He was a generous giver but believed that the Gospel taught such anonymity in giving that the "right hand should not know what the left hand is doing." He counseled that

businesses had a responsibility to give back to the communities that supported them. He was a respected industry and civic leader, the first Italian American elected to the Galveston city council, and honored by his contemporaries in the business community with the affectionate nickname, "Mr. Beachfront." In his honor, 39th Street was renamed Mike Gaido Boulevard. Mike's wife, "Kewpie," also supported the community in her own inimitable way at St. Mary's Hospital, St. Mary's Orphanage, and the Bishop's Palace. She is best remembered for her lifelong dedication to Galveston's oleanders. It is unlikely those who knew Mike Gaido best would characterize him as a liberal, but when the time was right at long last to put an end to segregated public dining in Galveston, Mike Gaido was determined to do what was right. Even after beachfront restaurants agreed to end desegregation on the Tuesday after Labor Day in 1962,

Gaido's was one of the few that did so. Without fanfare Mike Gaido sought out prominent local African Americans to join the Galveston Pelican Club. When his son Wayne's Drive Inn was boycotted in 1963 because it was the only beachfront drive-in to hire African American carhops, Mike Gaido shuttered the business rather than dismiss any of the staff. Though only a memory when Hurricane Ike struck the island in 2008, it was Mike Gaido's example of doing what was right that inspired his family to honor Galveston's first responders with a white tablecloth Shrimp Boil in the front parking lot a full two weeks before the restaurant had its utilities restored.

Mike and Kewpie Gaido had four children, Mickey, Wayne, Paulie, and Lynette, all of whom worked for their dad as kids. Lynette ultimately moved to Houston and became a translator and instructor in

Harry Rabe, Johnny Weismuller, Mike Gaido

Mandarin Chinese. Her three brothers chose to join the family business and build upon what Cinto and Mike had bequeathed to them. Mickey, who still manages to work seven days a week, was the steadying influence and acknowledged leader of his generation. An inexhaustible outdoorsman, he used his first-hand knowledge of the natural habitat and life cycles of shrimp, oysters, blue crabs, and local fish along with his extensive education in biology and chemistry to make certain that Gaido's served only the highest quality seafood day after day, year after year.

Mickey Gaido with Benno Deltz

It was Mickey, along with long time general manager Benno Deltz, who managed the "front of the house" and set new standards of excellence for service quality. Mickey, who continues to serve as the chairman of the board of a highly successful local bank was, not surprisingly, the third generation's financial planner, insurance analyst, and business prognosticator. His lifelong fascination with meteorology also made him the ultimate "in-house" weather forecaster, a critical skill in a business located in a resort community that is blue sky and temperature driven and located on a barrier island that has seen more than its fair share of tropical weather disturbances. Wayne Gaido, who chose to concentrate his efforts in the Pelican Club, was twice blessed. He possessed an unerring seasoning touch and the best palate of his generation, making him indispensable in recipe development as well as recipe rescue. Remarkably, however, he also had the personal warmth, genuine

humility, and "never met a stranger" attitude to make him, arguably, the most personable Gaido ever in the dining room, a singular distinction given his father and grandfather's people skills. It is a continuing tribute to his ability to please that guests still inquire, "Where's Wayne?" some two decades after his retirement. Last to join the family business, youngest brother Paulie found a home in Gaido's kitchens and happily spent his entire career there. Paulie had abiding respect for what his grandfather, father, and brothers had accomplished but nevertheless felt there was room for improvement and methodically set about raising the bar for every aspect of the restaurant's performance. It was Paulie who reworked every family recipe, maintaining that flavor consistency could only be achieved with scrupulous attention to measurement of ingredients and step-by-step incorporation. To ensure food quality he insisted that food preparation

track estimated customer counts and historical menu choices. He demanded that every entrée and even every side dish be cooked exclusively to order, a daunting task for a restaurant whose volume often exceeded 2,500 guests on a summer Saturday. It was Paulie who began the open-flame charcoal and iron skillet grilling of fresh fish. Convinced that training was essential to achieving consistent performance, he wrote training manuals for every employee classification in the kitchen and dining room. Honoring his father's example of giving back to the community, Paulie chose to be a part of Galveston's historic preservation renaissance through a number of projects through the years.

Harris Kempner, Paulie and Mary Kay Gaido, Michael Creamer, and David Brink at the helm of the sailing ship *Elissa*, 1984.

He was honored to participate in the hands-on restoration of St. Joseph's Church, the creation of Ashton Villa's multimedia presentation about the 1900 Storm, seawall building and grade raising, and the return of the sailing vessel *Elissa* to Galveston.

The torch is being passed to the fourth generation of the Gaido family, but the transition is not yet complete. It is too soon to know what their ultimate contribution will be, but they have certainly had an auspicious beginning. Although no-one in the first three generations had professional culinary training, three of Cinto's great-grandchildren—Kim, Casey, and Nick—are graduates of the Culinary Institute of America. Ritchie, Kim, Michael, and John all made solid contributions before changing careers. Especially significant was the innovation without loss of continuity provided by Fritz Gaido's grandson, Rick Gaido, during his tenure as general manager. The future seems especially bright given the commitment, enthusiasm, and culinary expertise of CIA graduates Nick and Casey Gaido, who currently share the helm of Gaido's in its second century of service.

Fritz, Mike, and S.J. Gaido

Wayne, Mickey, and Paulie Gaido

MIKE GAIDO BLVD 39th St

39th street, where Gaido's famous seafood restaurant currently resides, was renamed Mike Gaido Boulevard in the 1980s by the Galveston City Council in recognition of his many charitable acts. It was done at the request of city leaders and a community eager to give back to a "Mr. Beachfront" who had given so much to it.

WAITER'S JACKET

This notable wardrobe was worn by all Gaido's servers for more than three decades starting in 1970. The jacket design was made to replicate similar coats worn by waiters who participated in the same service at Murdoch's bath house a half century before them.

Roman De Los Santos, a customer favorite bartender at Gaido's since 1973.

Cocktails & After-Dinner Drinks

"Gaido's understands wine and its

relationship to food."

Cocktails & After-Dinner Drinks

Raspberry Lemon Drop

Peach Bellini

Rocket Man

Gaido's Bloody Mary

Brandy Milk Punch

The Wooden Shoe

Margarita

Voo Doo

Godiva Chocolate Martini

Pom-Tini

Malibu Mai Tai

Sazerac

Polar Bear

Castilla Coffee

Afternoon Delight

Wine

ENHANCING THE MEAL

For much of the first half of the twentieth century, *wine* was an afterthought at Gaido's. Jug wines included Manishewitz and Mogen David Kosher, along with Christian Brother's sauterne, burgundy, and chablis. The list of wines available by the bottle topped out at twenty. In the 1970s Americans began to pay more attention to wine, and Paulie Gaido realized that Gaido's needed not only to offer a more extensive wine selection but also to have someone on premises who understood wine and its relationship to food. Lorene Kemps became Gaido's first sommelier, and a twenty-year love affair began between Gaido's customers and Lorene and her wine.

Replacing Lorene was impossible, but finding someone to take over her work proved easier. Paulie asked his wife, Mary Kay, if she'd like to work at the restaurant, and her immediate response was, "No, thank you, you bring too much of your job home already." When, however, he told her that he'd like her to be the wine buyer, she said, "I'll start tomorrow." Mary Kay has been the wine buyer ever since and has embraced that role wholeheartedly—so much so that, when Hurricane Ike was approaching Galveston, and despite her husband Paulie's admonition that "it's only wine," she made trip after trip from the wine cellar to a "safe" location on the mainland until rising water closed the interstate highway.

Raspberry Lemon Drop

Raspberry Lemon Drop

Makes 1 drink

Sugar
2 whole lemons
1 ounce sweet-and-sour mix

½ ounce 2:1 simple syrup (see note)
1½ ounces Absolut Citron vodka
½ ounce Chambord

Dip the rim of a martini glass into water and then into sugar to coat the rim. Place the glass into the freezer until frosted.

Squeeze the lemons into a cocktail shaker, catching the seeds in a cheesecloth or bar strainer.

Add the sweet-and-sour mix, simple syrup and Absolut Citron.

Fill shaker to the top with ice. Shake to mix.

Strain the mixture into the frosted martini glass. Place a bar spoon upside down across the top of the glass. Pour the Chambord slowly and evenly over the spoon, allowing it to settle in a layer on top of the vodka mixture. Pour slowly so the Chambord doesn't mix with the rest of the drink.

Note: *Simple syrup is a basic sugar-and-water mixture used in drinks. To make it, stir granulated sugar into hot water in a saucepan over low heat until the sugar is dissolved; let cool. Syrup can be made in 1:1 ratio (one part sugar, one part water) or 2:1 ratio (two parts sugar to one part water). This recipe calls for 2:1 syrup.*

Peach Bellini

Makes 1 drink

1½ ounces prosecco
1 ounce peach schnapps

2½ ounces peach purée
10 ounces ice

Combine the prosecco, peach schnapps, peach purée and ice in a blender. Process until smooth.

Pour the mixture into a Champagne flute or cocktail glass and serve right away before the prosecco breaks down the ice.

Rocket Man

1/2 ounce light rum
1/2 ounce gin
1/2 ounce vodka
1/2 ounce Triple Sec

4 ounces sweet-and-sour mix
1 ounce lemon-lime soda
Lemon slice and lime slice
Additional lemon-lime soda

Combine the first six ingredients in a cocktail shaker; shake to blend.

Pour over ice in a large cocktail glass or hurricane glass.

Garnish with a lemon slice and a lime slice. Add a splash of lemon-lime soda.

Gaido's Bloody Mary

Makes 10 drinks

Salt
Pepper
7 1/2 cups tomato juice
1 cup tomato paste
1/2 cup Worcestershire sauce

1/2 tablespoon Tabasco sauce
1 cup lemon juice concentrate
1 3/4 cups vodka
10 celery stalks
2 limes, cut into wedges

Dip the rims of 10 glasses into water, then into salt and pepper to coat the rims.

Combine the next five ingredients in a large pitcher and mix well. Add the vodka and mix well.

Place a celery stick in each glass and fill three-fourths full of ice. Pour the Bloody Mary over the ice just before serving. Garnish each with a lime wedge.

Gaido's Bloody Mary's are made with very little spice in the base mix so that upon request patrons can finish theirs how they see fit, be it stuffed olives, horseradish, more lime, Tabasco, or all of the above. What we do ensure in the mix is a tomato paste so the body of the drink is full and not watered down.

KEWPIE GAIDO AND SEAGULL BREAD

All of her life "Kewpie" Gaido adored plants, especially her beloved oleanders, but her heart positively ached when she witnessed animal suffering. She was a tireless and often very vocal opponent of animal neglect and a two-legged nightmare for those engaged in animal cruelty. Each morning and evening until her death she fed the seawall seagulls, who recognized their benefactor and waited patiently for her to appear on the porch outside her apartment. In her memory, Gaido's kitchen fills bags with leftover house-baked bread and encourages Gaido's and Casey Gaido's guests to feed the seagulls in Kewpie's memory.

Brandy Milk Punch

1 1/4 ounces brandy
1/2 ounce dark crème de cacao
1/4 ounce 2:1 simple syrup (page 31)
5 ounces half-and-half
Cinnamon
Nutmeg

Combine brandy, crème de cacao, simple syrup and half-and-half in a cocktail shaker.

Shake to blend. Pour over ice in a glass. Garnish with a dash of cinnamon and a dash of nutmeg.

The Wooden Shoe

Makes 1 drink

1 1/4 ounces dark crème de cacao
3/4 ounce piña colada mix
1 ounce coconut liqueur
8 ounces Blue Bell vanilla ice cream
Whipped cream
Cinnamon

Combine crème de cacao, piña colada mix, coconut liqueur and ice cream in a blender. Process until smooth.

Pour into a glass. Top with whipped cream and garnish with a dash of cinnamon.

THE WOODEN SHOE

Famous for its ice cream desserts and drinks, Gaido's Wooden Shoe stands alone as the most popular of its kind. Commonly asked as to the origin of the unique name, the title was derived from a Dutch ship captain. The ship captain came into town while goods were being unloaded from his ship at the port of Galveston. The ship captain enthusiastically assisted in the choosing of liqueurs while dining at the bar the night the drink was created.

Margarita

Makes 10 drinks

Salt
2 (12-ounce) cans frozen limeade concentrate, partially thawed
4 cups Key lime juice
9³/4 ounces Triple Sec

2¹/2 cups water
13 ounces tequila
3¹/2 cups sugar
3 limes, cut into wedges

Dip the rims of cocktail glasses into water and then into salt to coat the rims.

Combine the limeade, Key lime juice, Triple Sec, water and tequila in a pitcher and mix well.

Pour in the sugar slowly, stirring to dissolve.

For each drink, combine 5 ounces of the limeade mixture with ice in a cocktail shaker. Shake vigorously to create a frothy, well-blended drink.

Pour into a prepared glass. Garnish with a lime wedge.

Voo Doo

Makes 1 drink

¹/2 ounce light rum
¹/2 ounce spiced rum
¹/2 ounce apricot brandy
3 ounces pineapple juice

2 ounces sweet-and-sour mix
1 splash grenadine
¹/2 ounce Myers's dark rum
Lime slices

Combine the light rum, spiced rum, apricot brandy, pineapple juice, sweet-and-sour mix and grenadine in a cocktail shaker. Shake a little to blend.

Fill a hurricane glass with ice. Pour the mixture over the ice. Top with the Myers's rum. Garnish with a lime slice.

JULIO YUCRA

Born in Bolivia and educated at the Conrad Hilton School of Restaurant and Hotel Management, Julio Yucra spent his entire professional career at the Pelican Club until his untimely death. He was a customer favorite from his very first day, which is hardly surprising given his genuine warmth, grace under fire, impeccable personal appearance, and seemingly effortless continental charm. Julio was an extraordinary host and for an entire generation symbolized the southern hospitality and personal attention that made the Pelican Club world famous. Though suffering from an incurable and painful illness, he nonetheless chose to "work the floor" until he was no longer able to stand. Astonishingly, throughout his ordeal he not only rejected self-pity but somehow found a way to smile. For the Gaido family and staff Julio was a one-of-a-kind comrade-at-arms, a once-in-a-lifetime blessing. He will never leave our thoughts, never leave our prayers, and never leave our hearts.

Richard Emerson, Lorene Kemps, and Julio Yucra

Godiva Chocolate Martini

Godiva Chocolate Martini

Makes 1 drink

Grated chocolate
1   ounce 3 Olive chocolate vodka
1½   ounces Godiva chocolate liqueur
1½   ounces half-and-half

Dip the rim of a martini glass into water and then into grated chocolate to coat the rim.

Combine the remaining ingredients in a cocktail shaker. Fill the shaker with ice.

Shake five to seven times to create a froth without watering down the martini.

Strain into the prepared glass.

Pom-Tini

Makes 1 drink

1½   ounces Absolut Citron vodka
3   ounces pomegranate juice
1   ounce sweet-and-sour mix
1   orange slice

Combine the vodka, pomegranate juice and sweet-and-sour mix in a cocktail shaker. Add ice and shake vigorously.

Strain into a frozen or chilled martini glass. Squeeze the orange slice into the glass. Garnish with the orange peel.

Malibu Mai Tai

Malibu Mai Tai

Makes 1 drink

1 1/4   ounces Malibu rum
2   ounces pineapple juice
2   ounces orange juice
1   splash grenadine

1/2   ounce Myers's dark rum
1   orange slice
1   maraschino cherry

Combine the Malibu rum, pineapple juice and orange juice in a cocktail shaker; stir to blend.

Place ice in a cocktail glass. Pour mixture over ice.

Layer the grenadine into a "sunrise effect" by pouring it over a spoon on the edge of the glass slowly, ensuring the grenadine falls to the bottom of the glass.

Top the drink with the Myers's dark rum, an orange slice and a maraschino cherry

Sazerac

Makes 1 drink

3/4   ounce 2:1 simple syrup (page 31)
3   dashes angostura bitters
2 1/2   ounces Hennessy cognac

1   splash Pernod
1   lemon twist

Chill a brandy snifter or a high ball glass with ice.

Combine the simple syrup and bitters in a glass. Add the cognac and ice; stir well.

Discard the ice in the brandy snifter.

Pour the Pernod into the glass and swirl it around; discard the Pernod.

Strain the drink into the chilled glass. Squeeze the lemon peel over the glass to give a lemon essence, not lemon flavor. Garnish with the lemon peel.

IKE RESPONDERS

On Thursday, September 18th, 2008, less than a week after the arrival of Hurricane Ike, Gaido's restaurant opened its doors to the first responders who so bravely helped in the aftermath. Without basic utilities, Gaido's trucked in butane, generators, bottled water, and most notably, linen tablecloths to provide the men and women a reminder of the common-day luxuries they had been without.

Polar Bear

Makes 10 drinks

1 whole pineapple
6 cups pineapple sherbet
2¹/₂ cups pineapple juice
2¹/₄ (15-ounce) cans Coco Lopez cream of coconut

Peel the pineapple and cut out the eyes. Cut the pineapple into wedges and cut a slit into each wedge so it can sit on the rim of a glass.

Combine the sherbet, pineapple juice and cream of coconut in a large blender. Process until smooth.

For each drink, fill a 14-ounce glass with ice. Combine the ice and 3³/₄ ounces of the pineapple mixture in a blender. Process until smooth.

Pour the mixture into the glass. Garnish with a pineapple wedge.

This nonalcoholic version of a Piña Colada is understandably a treat most enjoyed by the countless children who frequent with their parents. Popular enough to be called by its name, it is a unique and creamy mixture that has a strong coconut and fresh pineapple taste, bringing out the best of both. For those who prefer the adult version, feel free to add 1¹/₄ shots of any rum when blending the ice and mix together.

Castilla Coffee

Castilla Coffee

Makes 1 drink

$1/2$ ounce Triple Espresso vodka
$1/2$ ounce Bailey's Irish cream
$1/2$ ounce amaretto
2 ounces coffee
$1 1/2$ ounces foamed milk
Whipped cream
Cinnamon

Combine vodka, Irish cream, amaretto and coffee in an Irish coffee glass.

Top with foamed milk, whipped cream and cinnamon.

Afternoon Delight

Makes 1 drink

4 scoops chocolate ice cream
$1 1/4$ ounces amaretto
Whipped cream

Combine the ice cream and amaretto in a blender. Process until smooth.

Pour into a cocktail glass. Top with whipped cream.

Executive chef Zach McClendon inspects a daily shipment of oysters.

Appetizers

"Flavor is key to bringing

the palate back."

Appetizers

Iced Shrimp

Shrimp Peques

Gaido's Crab Cakes

Crab Meat Cheesecake

Coconut Tuna Ceviche

"Everything Bagel" Tuna

Angels on Horseback

Surf-n-Turf Kabobs

Kobe Sliders

Elements of Great Cuisine
FLAVOR

Three underlying principles have been instilled in the countless people who have built Gaido's cuisine over the last century: concentration of FLAVOR, built from solid FOUNDATIONS and derived from the FRESHEST ingredients possible.

Flavor is key to bringing the palate back. Patience is critical in ensuring quality flavor. If you rush the process the end product will suffer.

Gaido's kitchen is filled with recipes that require multiple steps. These extra steps are essential to replicating customer favorites in your kitchen. Starting from scratch is essential—no matter how closely one follows the recipe for tartar sauce found in this book, the result won't be the same unless the mayonnaise used is made from scratch. The recipes found in this book are the exact recipes used at Gaido's, reduced to satisfy a household kitchen.

Famous for their soldier-like posture, Gaido's Iced Shrimp have been the favored vehicle for sampling Gaido's cocktail, tartar, and rémoulade sauces. While the procedure is a time-consuming and complicated endeavor, Gaido's chefs seem more than happy to make them in hopes that they can answer a common customer inquiry as to how the shrimp came about their shape. "With a slight tap of the pan and call to attention, the shrimp are merely scared straight."

Iced Shrimp

Makes 5 or 6 servings

Shrimp Shocking Solution
2   quarts ice
2   quarts water
2   tablespoons liquid crab boil
2   tablespoons hot pepper sauce
2   tablespoons salt

Shrimp and Assembly
40   (16- to 20-count) jumbo shrimp,
     peeled, deveined
6   ounces Cocktail Sauce
     (page 68)
6   ounces Rémoulade Sauce
     (page 71)

For the Shrimp Shocking Solution, combine the ice, water, crab boil, pepper sauce and salt in a bowl.

For the Shrimp, close the shrimp and arrange them folded side down, packed very tightly on a perforated pan such as a steamer pan. Set a pan with 5 pounds of weight on top of the shrimp to prevent movement. Lower the pans into a pot of boiling water. Cook the shrimp for 8 minutes.

Remove the shrimp to the Shrimp Shocking Solution and let stand for 20 minutes; drain.

Chill in the refrigerator or serve immediately sprinkled with shaved ice. Serve with Cocktail Sauce and Rémoulade Sauce.

This recipe calls for 40 jumbo shrimp to fill an 9x11½-inch pan to ensure the shrimp won't spread apart.

Shrimp Peques

Makes 1 serving

Brown Sugar Glaze

1   cup packed brown sugar
4   tablespoons lemon juice
2   tablespoons molasses
1   tablespoon honey
1   teaspoon chipotle base
    (optional)

Shrimp

7   jumbo shrimp
2   cups bread crumbs
1/2 cup finely shredded Cheddar-
    Jack cheese
1   teaspoon seasoned salt
7   whole jalapeño peppers, julienned
7   bacon strips

For the Brown Sugar Glaze, combine the sugar, lemon juice, molasses, honey and chipotle base in a saucepan. Bring to a boil. Remove from heat and cool to room temperature.

For the Shrimp, peel, devein and butterfly the shrimp. Preheat the oven to 350 degrees.

Combine the bread crumbs and cheese. Divide the mixture into seven 1-ounce portions and shape into oblongs around slivers of jalapeño.

Stuff the mixture into the belly side of the shrimp. Wrap each stuffed shrimp tightly with a piece of bacon.

Arrange the shrimp on a baking sheet. Bake for 15 minutes.

Coat the shrimp with Brown Sugar Glaze and bake for 5 minutes longer.

While easier to deep-fry shrimp brochette, this is frowned upon in Gaido's kitchen. The shrimp take on flavors from other foods that may have been cooked in the fryer. Shrimp Peques are started on the grill to acquire a charcoal taste and then moved to the oven to be cooked 90 percent of the way, only to be removed once more and coated in the brown sugar glaze and then finished in the oven. The window of time for the shrimp and bacon to be neither under- nor overcooked is very narrow.

JAMES PEQUES

Raised on the plains of West Texas, Galveston was James Peques' first stop after a four-year tour of duty in the United States Army. His career at Gaido's began as an apprentice to Luther Cotton, Gaido's legendary Fry Station Chef. When at last the opportunity came to assume command of the "hot corner," his performance was exceptional, drawing comparisons to his retired tutor and mentor. Years later, when Wade Watkins succeeded Charles Brooks as Executive Chef, James "Piggy" Peques left the front line to become Wade's assistant, strong right arm, and heir apparent. Warm and funny, with the lyrics of a country song or the play-by-play of a Monday night football game often on his lips, he was nonetheless all business when it was time to do business. Built like an NFL linebacker and able to assume an intimidating demeanor when the occasion demanded, he was the perfect gatekeeper for Gaido's kitchen deliveries. He knew fresh seafood and was absolutely determined that Gaido's standards of quality could not and would not be compromised. Shrimpers, fishermen, and all manner of seafood purveyors understood that sneaking less than the best past "Mr. Piggy" was like trying to sneak the rising sun past a rooster. He left nine children who loved him dearly and a restaurant family who will never forget him.

Gaido's Crab Cakes

Makes 10 Servings

Cognac Sauce

1   tablespoon shallots, minced

1/2   quart heavy cream

1/2   teaspoon lobster base

5   tablespoons light brown sugar

5   whole sage leaves

1/2   cup cognac

Crab Cakes

4   tablespoons Gaido's Mayonnaise (page 70)

5   teaspoons prepared Dijon mustard

5   teaspoons Worcestershire sauce

3   tablespoons Old Bay seasoning

5   tablespoons unsalted butter, softened

5   teaspoons half-and-half

5   tablespoons shallots, minced

3   eggs

3   cups fresh bread crumbs

2 1/2   pounds jumbo lump crab meat, divided

Vegetable oil for searing

For the Cognac Sauce, sweat the shallots in a saucepan until translucent. Add the cream, lobster base, brown sugar and sage. Cook until reduced by half. Strain through a chinois or cheesecloth. The sauce should easily coat a spoon. Bring the cognac to a boil in a medium saucepan and cook until reduced by half. Combine both sauces; strain.

For the Crab Cakes, preheat the oven to 350 degrees. Combine the mayonnaise, mustard, Worcestershire sauce, Old Bay, butter, half-and-half, shallots and eggs in a bowl; mix well. Add the bread crumbs and mix until the crumbs are saturated.

Fold 2 pounds of the crab meat into the mixture and mix gently to combine.

Coat ten 4-ounce baking cups with nonstick cooking spray. Divide the mixture evenly among the cups. Bake for 15 minutes. Remove the cakes from the baking cups.

Sear the crab cakes in a little oil in a sauté pan over high heat until light brown. Turn and sear the other side.

Top each crab cake with two or three pieces of lump crab meat. Drizzle with 1/8 cup of Cognac Sauce.

Crab Meat Cheesecake

Makes 10 servings

Almond Shortbread Crust

1 1/2 cups almonds
1 1/4 cups all-purpose flour
1/2 cup sugar
1 cup salted butter
1 egg, beaten

Crab Meat Cheesecake

16 ounces cream cheese
16 ounces mascarpone cheese
1/4 cup sugar
4 eggs
2 teaspoons Dijon mustard
6 tablespoons dry sherry
1 cup shallots, diced
Vegetable oil for sautéing
2 pounds lump crab meat
1 tablespoon salt
1/2 tablespoon pepper
Meunière Sauce (at right)
2 1/4 cups unsalted butter

For the Almond Shortbread Crust, preheat the oven to 350 degrees. Toast the almonds on a baking sheet for 10 minutes. Grind the almonds in a food processor. Increase the oven temperature to 375 degrees.

Combine the almonds, flour and sugar in a bowl; mix well.

Heat the butter in a saucepan over medium heat until it browns; cool slightly. Add the butter and egg to the flour mixture and mix well. Spread the mixture over the bottom and up the side of a 9-inch springform pan. Bake for 15 minutes; let cool.

For the Crab Meat Cheesecake, beat the cream cheese, mascarpone cheese and sugar in a mixing bowl until smooth. Add the eggs and mustard; mix well.

Heat the sherry in a saucepan until reduced to 1/4 cup. Add to the cream cheese mixture.

Sauté the shallots in a little oil in a sauté pan until translucent. Add to the filling mixture. Fold in the crab meat. Season with salt and pepper.

Wrap foil around the outside of the springform pan; crimp to seal. Spoon the filling into the cooled crust. Set the springform pan in a larger baking pan and add water to the larger pan to come halfway up the side of the pan. Bake for 1 1/2 hours.

Cut the cheesecake into 10 slices. For each slice, combine 2 tablespoons of the Meunière Sauce and 4 tablespoons of the butter in a saucepan. Cook until the butter melts, stirring; drizzle over the cheesecake.

Meunière Sauce

Makes 1 quart

1/2	cup salted butter		1/2	onion, chopped
1/2	cup all-purpose flour		3	garlic cloves, minced
1	quart Worcestershire sauce		1/4	teaspoon pepper
4	teaspoons Herb Mixture (page 73)			

Melt the butter in a large saucepan over medium heat. Add the flour and cook until the mixture is the color of a dark penny, stirring constantly to prevent scorching.

Whisk in the Worcestershire sauce, Herb Mixture, onion, garlic and pepper. Simmer for 10 minutes; pour through a strainer.

For use in other recipes than Crab Meat Cheesecake, finish with 2 tablespoons butter per 1 tablespoon of Meunière Sauce.

Coconut Tuna Ceviche

Makes 3 or 4 servings

1	(12-ounce) can cream of coconut		1	tablespoon cilantro leaves
1 1/2	cups rice wine vinegar		3/4	cup diced red onion
1/2	teaspoon ground red pepper		3/4	cup diced red bell pepper
1/2	teaspoon ground cumin		1 1/2	pounds fresh tuna, diced
1/2	teaspoon ground cloves			Pinch of lemon zest

Combine the cream of coconut and vinegar in a blender or food processor; process until well blended. Add the pepper, cumin, cloves and cilantro; process for 30 seconds. Combine the

mixture with the onion and red bell pepper in a large bowl.

Add the tuna to the coconut mixture; let stand 5 minutes.

Top with the lemon zest. Refrigerate until chilled.

"Everything Bagel" Tuna

Makes 4 servings

Wasabi

2 teaspoons water
3 teaspoons wasabi powder
1/2 teaspoon salt
1/4 teaspoon ground ginger
3 tablespoons heavy cream

Everything Coating and Assembly

1/2 cup sesame seeds
1/4 cup poppy seeds
3 tablespoons garlic powder
1 1/2 tablespoons onion powder
1/4 teaspoon pepper
4 (4-ounce) tuna steaks
Butter for sautéing

For the Wasabi, combine the water, wasabi powder, salt and ginger in a bowl to form a paste. Let stand for 5 minutes. Blend in the heavy cream until smooth.

For the Everything Coating, combine the seeds, garlic powder, onion powder and pepper in a bowl.

Coat the tuna steaks with the Everything Coating.

Sear the tuna in butter in a large sauté pan.

Slice into 1/4-inch strips and fan tuna over a serving plate.

Serve the tuna topped with Wasabi.

Angels on Horseback

Makes 8 servings

Smoked Gouda Cream Sauce
1/2 cup heavy cream
2 ounces smoked Gouda cheese

Oysters and Assembly
8 (2-inch) squares puff pastry
8 oysters, shucked
4 bacon slices, cut in half
6 tablespoons flour
4 tablespoons butter

For the Smoked Gouda Cream Sauce, heat the cream in a saucepan. Add the cheese and cook until cheese is melted, stirring; strain.

For the Oysters, score each square of puff pastry on all sides 1/4 inch from the edge. Bake according to the package directions; let cool.

Wrap each oyster with a piece of bacon. Secure with a wooden pick. Dust oysters in flour. Heat the butter in a sauté pan. Sauté the oysters until the bacon is thoroughly cooked.

Remove and reserve the puffed center portion of each puff pastry square. Place an oyster on each pastry. Drizzle with 1 tablespoon of the sauce.

Replace the reserved puff pastry tops. Serve hot.

Surf-n-Turf Kabobs

Makes 1 serving

Marinade

1 ½ cups pineapple juice

Juice of 3 limes

1 tablespoon ground ginger

¼ cup cilantro

⅓ cup honey

1 teaspoon salt

½ teaspoon pepper

Assembly for Each Serving

2 medium cubes beef

4 jumbo shrimp, peeled

2 ounces butter for sautéing

2 pineapple slices, grilled

Cilantro sprigs

2 skewers

For the marinade, combine all the marinade ingredients in a large shallow dish; mix well.

For the Assembly, thread a beef cube onto each skewer. Thread a shrimp each onto each skewer. Place the beef and shrimp skewers in the marinade; marinate for 5 to 7 minutes.

Sauté the beef and shrimp skewers in butter in a large sauté pan for 1 minute on each side.

Overlap pineapple slices on a serving plate. Top with the beef and shrimp, crisscrossing the skewers.

Garnish with cilantro.

Kobe Sliders

Makes 12 patties

Caramelized Onions

3   yellow onions, sliced

5   tablespoons plus 1 teaspoon butter

1   tablespoon salt

1/2   tablespoon pepper

Blue Cheese Sauce

9   ounces blue cheese crumbles

3   cups heavy cream

Sliders

1   pound ground Kobe beef

1   cup fresh bread crumbs

2   eggs

1/2   cup Parmesan cheese

1   tablespoon chopped parsley

1/8   small onion, grated

2   garlic cloves, minced

1/3   cup butter, cut into 1/4-inch cubes

1/2   teaspoon nutmeg

1/2   tablespoon salt

1   teaspoon pepper

Assembly

French bread, cut into 12 (1/4-inch) slices

Crispy bacon bits

Chopped parsley

For the Caramelized Onions, combine the onions, butter, salt and pepper in a sauté pan. Cook over medium heat until onions are caramelized and translucent.

For the Blue Cheese Sauce, combine the cheese and cream in a small saucepan over medium heat. Cook until the cheese is melted and cream is reduced by half, stirring often.

For the Sliders, combine all Slider ingredients in a large bowl; mix well. Shape 1-ounce portions into patties.

Cook the patties in a large sauté pan over medium to medium-high heat for 2 minutes on each side.

For the Assembly, toast the bread slices. Top each slice with Caramelized Onions and Blue Cheese Sauce. Garnish with bacon bits and parsley.

Sauces, Stocks & Seasonings

"The foundations distinguish great food

from merely good food."

Sauces, Stocks & Seasonings

Asiago Sauce

Cocktail Sauce

Creamy Onion Garlic Dressing

Thousand Island Dressing

Honey Pecan Vinaigrette

Gaido's Mayonnaise

Rémoulade Sauce

Tartar Sauce

Charcoal Seasoning

Herb Mixture

Chicken Stock

Elements of Great Cuisine
F O U N D A T I O N S

Often referred to as fonds de cuisine, or the *foundations* of cooking, stocks are what distinguish great chefs from good chefs and, ultimately, great food from merely good food. The purpose of any stock is to extract flavor from a bone, vegetable, or other ingredient that might not otherwise be captured. They are utilized in almost all aspects of cooking, from soups to stocks to risotto. The time spent making a proper stock or base will undoubtedly be revealed in the final dish.

Many recipes in this book call for a base. Put most simply, a base, demi-glace, or any fortified stock is the result of taking the derivative from a previous stock or sauce and repeating the process with thickeners and aromatics until the desired consistency is achieved.

These foundations are a recipe's lasting legacy. The work required to build the stocks and fortify the sauces that go into dishes far surpasses that of any other element in cooking. There is, however, no greater return. Knowing that a homemade base or sauce will require much more time than many are able to commit, please feel free to look to outside resources for alternatives. Commercial bases are an option that can be found at certain grocers as well as on line. Most bases will be found in powder form; look for those made from meats, bones, and vegetables that are low in high-sodium ingredients.

Asiago Sauce

Makes 1 1/2 quarts

4   tablespoons butter
1/3   cup all-purpose flour
1/2   cup half-and-half
1 2/3   cups heavy cream

1   tablespoon chicken base
4   ounces shredded asiago cheese
4   ounces grated Parmesan cheese

Melt the butter in a saucepan over low heat. Stir in the flour and cook for 4 to 10 minutes to make a light blonde roux.

Add the half-and-half, cream and chicken base, stirring constantly to prevent lumps.

Add the cheeses gradually, mixing with a wire whisk.

Increase the temperature and bring to a boil. Keep at a boil until the sauce coats the back of a spoon.

Cocktail Sauce

Makes 3 1/2 cups

1 3/4   cups ketchup
1   cup (scant) chili sauce
1   tablespoon Worcestershire sauce
3   tablespoons horseradish

2   teaspoons Louisiana hot pepper sauce
4   teaspoons lemon juice

Combine the ketchup and chili sauce in a bowl; mix well.

Add the Worcestershire sauce, horseradish, hot sauce and lemon juice; mix well.

Our Cocktail Sauce is distinctive for several reasons, thicker than most with a distinctive flavor due to the chili sauce to tomato ketchup ratio, and a generous helping of horseradish and lemon juice.

Creamy Onion Garlic Dressing

2	cups Gaido's Mayonnaise (page 70)		1	teaspoon white pepper
¹/₄	cup onion juice		5	teaspoons finely chopped garlic
3	tablespoons frozen lemon juice		2	tablespoons red wine vinegar
³/₄	teaspoon salt		¹/₄	teaspoon paprika

Combine all ingredients in a large mixing bowl.

Mix at low speed until well blended.

Chill in the refrigerator for up to 2 weeks.

Thousand Island Dressing

Makes 3 cups

6	tablespoons sweet pickle relish		¹/₂	cup chili sauce
1	celery stalk		1¹/₂	tablespoons ketchup
2	cups Gaido's Mayonnaise (page 70)			

Drain the relish in a strainer.

Remove the strings from the celery. Chop the celery fine; squeeze dry.

Combine all ingredients in a mixing bowl; mix well.

Refrigerate until ready to use.

Honey Pecan Vinaigrette

Makes 1 quart

1/2	cup red wine vinegar
2	cups vegetable oil
4	tablespoons spicy brown mustard
1/2	cup plus 2 tablespoons honey
2	teaspoons oregano

2	teaspoons basil
1	teaspoon salt
1	teaspoon pepper
1	garlic clove, minced
1/2	cup pecan pieces, toasted

Combine the vinegar, oil, mustard, honey, oregano, basil, salt and pepper in a large bowl and whisk to blend thoroughly.

Add the garlic and toasted pecans and whisk to mix thoroughly.

Gaido's Mayonnaise

Makes 2³/₄ cups

5	egg yolks
1	tablespoon dry mustard
2¹/₄	cups vegetable oil, divided
2	to 2¹/₂ tablespoons white vinegar, divided

2	teaspoons salt
4	teaspoons sugar
2	teaspoons white pepper

Combine the egg yolks and dry mustard in a small mixing bowl. Beat until well blended.

Add 2 tablespoons of the oil gradually, beating constantly.

Add 2 more tablespoons of oil; mix well. Continue adding small amounts of oil, beating constantly.

When 1 cup of the oil has been added, add 1 to 1¹/₂ tablespoons of the vinegar; mix well.

Continue adding small amounts of oil with the mixer running until all the oil is used. Add the salt, sugar and white pepper; mix well.

Add the remaining 1 tablespoon vinegar; mix well. Chill in the refrigerator for up to 2 weeks.

Rémoulade Sauce

Makes about 2¹/₂ cups

3 green onions
¹/₃ cup fresh parsley
1 tablespoon capers, drained
5 tablespoons dill pickle relish, drained
1 ounce anchovies, drained
2 cups Gaido's Mayonnaise (at left)
4 tablespoons Creole mustard
1 teaspoon paprika
¹/₂ teaspoon white pepper

Grind the green onions, parsley, capers, relish and anchovies in a blender or food processor.

Place the mayonnaise in the bowl of a mixer.

Add the Creole mustard, paprika and white pepper; mix on medium speed.

Fold in the green onion mixture

Gaido's Rémoulade Sauce is arguably the most famous sauce produced by the Gaido family. The key ingredients that separate it from some other rémoulades you will find in New Orleans and other fine seafood restaurants are the anchovies and the Creole mustard. This is one recipe that we would urge you not to modify. If there is a perfect Gaido's summertime meal, it would be one with iced jumbo lump crab, boiled Gulf shrimp, saltine crackers, and our Rémoulade Sauce.

Tartar Sauce

Makes 6 cups

1 cup parsley
2 pounds yellow onions
5 cups Gaido's Mayonnaise
(page 70)

1 1/2 cups dill pickle relish, drained
1/2 teaspoon white pepper
1/2 teaspoon salt

Grind the parsley; wrap in a clean kitchen towel and press out the moisture.

Grind the onions. Drain the juice, reserving 1 tablespoon. Wrap the onions in a clean kitchen towel and press out the moisture.

Put the mayonnaise in a mixing bowl. Add the parsley, onions, relish, white pepper, salt and reserved onion juice; mix well.

Gaido's Tartar Sauce was created with the idea that it had to stand up to many rich seasonings for which it is so often used as a condiment. For this reason, the recipe is best when the mayonnaise is homemade.

Charcoal Seasoning

Makes about 1 pound

7 ounces paprika
3 ounces onion powder
2 ounces pepper

3 ounces marjoram
3 tablespoons salt

Combine the paprika, onion powder, pepper, marjoram and salt in a bowl; mix well.

Store at room temperature for up to 1 month.

Herb Mixture

Makes about 2 pounds

1	ounce (4 sprigs) fresh rosemary
1/2	ounce (1/4 bunch) fresh parsley
2	ounces (1 bunch) fresh basil
2	teaspoons fresh garlic, chopped
2	ounces garlic powder

1	ounce dried oregano
1/4	ounce red pepper flakes
1/2	ounce salt
1/2	ounce pepper

Wash the fresh herbs and dry thoroughly. Remove the leaves from the stems.

Combine the rosemary, parsley, basil, fresh garlic, garlic powder, oregano, red pepper flakes, salt and pepper in a food processor.

Process for 1 to 2 minutes until finely ground.

Chill in the refrigerator for up to 2 weeks.

Chicken Stock

Makes 2 1/2 quarts

3	pounds chicken pieces
1	onion, coarsely chopped
2	carrots, peeled, coarsely chopped
2	celery stalks, sliced

3	thyme sprigs
1	bay leaf
1	teaspoon salt
1/4	teaspoon black peppercorns
12	cups water

Combine the chicken, onion, carrots, celery, thyme, bay leaf, salt, peppercorns and water in a large stockpot. Bring to a simmer over high heat. Skim fat from the surface as it rises.

Reduce the heat to low. Set the pot halfway off the heat. Simmer

for 2 to 4 hours, skimming the fat from the surface.

Pour the stock through a strainer to remove the solids. Then pour it through a chinois or cheesecloth for a smooth texture. Store in the refrigerator for up to 4 days.

Soups, Salads & Side Dishes

"There is simply no substitute

for freshness."

Soups, Salads & Side Dishes

Soups & Salads

Watkins' Bisque

Crawfish Étoufée

Turkey Soup

Brooks' Gumbo

Southwest Butternut Squash Soup

Tortilla Soup

Shrimp Salad

Heirloom Salad

Glazed Pear Salad

Side Dishes

Au Gratin Potatoes

Mashed Sweet Potatoes

Creamed Spinach

Brentwood Polenta

Gorgonzola Grits

Truffled Mac & Cheese

The Elements of Great Cuisine
FRESHNESS

The third pillar of great cuisine is *freshness*. To make a lasting impression, your focus should be on creating a unique experience for your guests. In cuisine, this can only be achieved by using the freshest ingredients possible—there is simply no substitute for freshness.

The qualities that make food vibrant—the crackling of a freshly baked baguette, the shine of a newly filleted piece of fish, the smell of a soup coming to a boil for the first time—are not merely a feature but the *purpose* of great cuisine. With freshness, there is never a need to disguise or cover the element that should be on the forefront. To bake bread daily and make soups from scratch requires little more than the will to do so.

WADE WATKINS

A native Texan from Leon County, Wade Watkins came east to Galveston in 1948 after a start in the food service industry in San Antonio. Employed at the Buccaneer Hotel, he took a chance by joining Gaido's knowing that he might be laid off during the off-season. He not only survived that first winter but soon became an indispensable part of the kitchen and ultimately Gaido's Executive Chef. His exemplary forty-four–year career overlapped three generations of the Gaido family. Possessed of imposing physical stature, massive hands, rugged good looks, a warm smile, and an easy laugh, he was a natural leader. Through his leadership and by his example, Gaido's kitchen reflected his own performance and work ethic: Consistent, Reliable, Inexhaustible. Affectionately and respectfully known throughout his career as "Big Daddy," his influence endures through his recipes, especially his famous Bisque.

Watkins' Bisque

2   pounds onions, diced
Vegetable oil
5   tablespoons margarine
1   cup water
1½   pounds tomatoes, chopped
½   pound carrots, diced

4   cups heavy cream
2½   ounces lobster base
¾   teaspoon cayenne pepper
¾   teaspoon white pepper
Kitchen Bouquet to taste

Sweat the onions in a little oil in a large saucepan over medium heat for 20 minutes or until cooked through.

Add the margarine, water, tomatoes and carrots and cook for 30 minutes or until the vegetables are tender.

Place the mixture in a food processor; process to a smooth purée. Press through a fine mesh strainer into a large clean saucepan; discard the solids and fiber in the strainer.

Add the cream, lobster base, cayenne pepper, white pepper and Kitchen Bouquet to the mixture. Bring to a boil, stirring to blend. Simmer for 25 minutes to reduce to 6 cups. Strain before serving.

Variation: *Add 2 ounces cooked shrimp, lobster, or crab per serving.*

At the request of Paulie Gaido, Wade Watkins and Tom Ponzini created a bisque that had no other thickener than the tomatoes, carrots, and onions cooked into a dry, paste-like consistency. Brought back up with heavy cream, bisque should be handled with care; it will break if heated too rapidly and scorch if not constantly stirred.

Crawfish Étouffée

Makes 4 to 5 servings

8	ounces clarified butter		4	cups water
1¹/₂	cups all-purpose flour		1	cup heavy cream
6	tablespoons diced yellow onion			Pinch of white pepper
6	tablespoons diced green bell pepper		1¹/₂	tablespoons salt
6	tablespoons diced celery		¹/₂	teaspoon lemon zest
1¹/₄	pounds frozen crawfish tails			Pinch of paprika
¹/₂	tablespoon tomato paste			Pinch of thyme
2	cups cognac			Pinch of minced bay leaves
1	tablespoon seafood base		¹/₂	bunch parsley, chopped
				Hot cooked white rice (optional)

———

Heat the butter with the flour in a large saucepan over medium heat. Cook until the mixture is the color of a dark penny, stirring constantly.

Add the onion, bell pepper and celery and sweat the "holy trinity" of vegetables for 5 minutes. Turn the heat to medium-low and add the frozen crawfish and tomato paste. Cover the pan to "suffocate" the mixture for 30 minutes.

Heat the cognac in a small saucepan. Ignite it carefully with a long match. Let the flames reduce the cognac volume by half.

Combine the seafood base and water in a saucepan. Simmer over medium heat until base is dissolved. Add the cognac.

Add the cognac mixture, cream, white pepper, salt, lemon zest, paprika, thyme, bay leaves and parsley to the crawfish mixture and stir to combine.

Serve over hot cooked rice, if desired.

Turkey Soup

Makes 8 to 10 (8-ounce) servings

Vegetable Base
1 onion, chopped
2 large carrots, sliced
2 celery stalks, chopped
4 tablespoons butter
2 cups Chicken Stock (page 73)
Dash of thyme
1 bay leaf
6 sprigs parsley, chopped

Turkey Stock
8 cups water
4 tablespoons Vegetable Base

2 tablespoons chopped parsley
1/4 teaspoon thyme
1 bay leaf
1/2 teaspoon white pepper
1/2 teaspoon onion powder
1 turkey carcass, breast and back

Soup
6 tablespoons butter
12 tablespoons all-purpose flour
1 1/2 cups heavy cream
2 1/2 cups shredded turkey
1 teaspoon salt (optional)

For the Vegetable Base, sauté the onion, carrots, and celery in the butter until the onion is translucent. Add the Chicken Stock, thyme, bay leaf and parsley. Simmer until the liquid is evaporated. Be careful to not scorch the base. Discard the bay leaf. Purée the Base in a blender until smooth.

For the Turkey Stock, combine the stock ingredients in a pot. Bring to a boil; simmer for 1 hour. Strain into a clean pot.

For the Soup, heat the butter with the flour. Cook until the mixture thickens and forms a light brown roux, stirring constantly. Add the turkey stock. Bring to a boil over medium heat. Stir in the cream slowly. Add the turkey. Add salt if needed.

The Gaido family has always been well aware that employment in the hospitality business requires that the Gaido family and staff alike be separated from their families during holidays, especially on Thanksgiving Day and Christmas Eve. Accordingly, Gaido's has long provided Thanksgiving eve and Christmas holiday luncheons for not only the entire staff but their extended families as well. The turkey soup prepared especially for these luncheons became so popular that it earned a place on Gaido's menu during all of Thanksgiving week and throughout the Christmas holidays

CHARLES BROOKS

A native of Louisiana, Charles moved to Galveston at an early age. He worked at 38th and Seawall Boulevard at Deppen's Drive Inn before joining the Armed Forces for WWII. Discharged in 1945, he began a distinguished half-century career with the Gaido family. Respected and admired in the community for his character and success and loved by the extended family that he mentored and sustained, he was known simply as "Chef" to the thousands employed at Gaido's during his remarkable tenure. Soft spoken and slow to anger, but unquestionably in command, his influence endures through his recipes, especially his famous Seafood Gumbo.

A customer favorite for many years, our gumbo has been universally praised as well as scrutinized for it's not being in keeping with the Cajun style of southwest Louisiana. Created by chef Charles Brooks, a native of Thibodeaux, Louisiana, his has a substantially thicker consistency than most traditional gumbos.

Paulie Gaido and Charles Brooks

Brooks' Gumbo

Makes 10 to 12 (8-ounce) servings

8	tablespoons butter	1	teaspoon hot pepper sauce
1	cup all-purpose flour	2	teaspoons Worcestershire sauce
1	large yellow onion, finely chopped	3½	ounces chicken base
2	bell peppers, finely chopped	1	tablespoon gumbo filé
4	stalks celery	1	(3-ounce) bag crab boil
2½	cups chopped okra	1	tablespoon salt
15	cups water	20	to 24 ounces boiled shrimp or shredded cooked chicken
1	tablespoon tomato paste	2½	to 3 cups hot cooked rice
2	teaspoons pepper		

Heat the butter with the flour in a large stockpot over medium heat. Cook until the roux is the color of a dark penny, stirring constantly.

Sweat the onions in a large saucepan over medium-low heat to release their liquid. Cook until the liquid evaporates and the onions are caramelized.

Add the peppers and celery. Cook for 5 minutes. Add the roux and cook for 5 minutes longer.

Add the okra and 10 cups of the water. Bring to a simmer and cook until the okra falls apart.

Add the tomato paste, pepper, hot sauce, Worcestershire sauce and chicken base. Bring to a boil and slowly add the filé. Cook for 30 minutes.

Simmer the crab boil in the remaining 5 cups water for 5 minutes; discard the bag.

Add 2 ounces shrimp or chicken and 2 ounces rice to each serving.

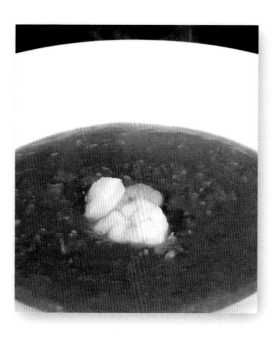

Southwest Butternut Squash Soup

Makes 6 (8-ounce) servings

Shrimp Salsa

1/3	cup diced yellow onion
1/4	cup diced red bell pepper
1/4	cup diced tomato
1/2	avocado, diced
1/4	cup cooked shrimp
1	tablespoon finely chopped cilantro
1	teaspoon lemon juice

Pinch of salt
Pinch of pepper

Squash Soup

1/3	cup diced yellow onion
1/3	cup diced celery
1/4	cup diced red bell pepper
1	pound butternut squash, peeled, diced
1	garlic clove, minced
2	tablespoons olive oil
2	cups Chicken Stock (page 73)
1	cup water
1	tablespoon ground cumin
1	tablespoon cinnamon
1	tablespoon nutmeg
2	tablespoons light brown sugar
1/2	cup heavy cream
1/2	teaspoon salt
1/2	teaspoon pepper

For the Shrimp Salsa, combine all salsa ingredients in a bowl. Refrigerate for 1 hour.

For the Squash Soup, sauté the onion, celery, bell pepper, squash and garlic in the olive oil in a large saucepan until tender.

Add the Chicken Stock, water, cumin, cinnamon, nutmeg and brown sugar. Simmer for 30 minutes.

Purée the mixture in a blender or food processor, or with an immersion blender, until smooth. Add the cream, salt and pepper. Cook until thoroughly heated.

Spoon 1 tablespoon of Salsa into a cup or bowl. Fill with Soup.

Tortilla Soup

Makes 8 servings

24 ounces canned Great Northern beans
16 ounces canned sweet corn
6 cups water
2 tablespoons chicken base
1 teaspoon chili powder
1 teaspoon paprika
1 teaspoon cumin
8 ounces Cheddar-Jack cheese, shredded
3 large corn tortillas (optional)
Vegetable oil for frying (optional)

Drain and rinse beans. Purée half the beans in a blender.

Drain the corn, reserving liquid. Purée half the corn in a blender.

Combine the puréed beans, puréed corn and water in a large saucepan. Add the whole beans and corn, reserved corn liquid, chicken base, chili powder, paprika and cumin. Bring to a boil. Reduce the heat to low and simmer for 10 minutes.

Add the cheese and cook for 3 to 5 minutes or until the cheese is melted, stirring.

Cut the tortillas into long thin strips. Fry in vegetable oil. Garnish the soup with tortilla strips to serve.

Shrimp Salad

2 cups (scant) diced celery
2 cups (scant) diced onion
6 hard-cooked eggs, diced
2 cups small shrimp, peeled, deveined, boiled
1 teaspoon white pepper

1 teaspoon salt
1/2 tablespoon dried basil
8 ounces Rémoulade Sauce (page 71)
Mixed spring greens

Sauté the celery and onion in a dry sauté pan until translucent; let cool.

Combine the celery, onion, eggs, shrimp, white pepper, salt and basil in a large mixing bowl.

Chill in the refrigerator until ready to serve.

To serve, add the Rémoulade Sauce and mix well. Serve over a bed of mixed spring greens.

Croutons made fresh daily at Gaido's

Heirloom Salad

Makes 4 servings

Balsamic Glaze

1   cup aged balsamic vinegar

Salad

4   heirloom tomatoes

3   fresh mozzarella balls

12   fresh basil leaves or sprigs

1   teaspoon salt

1   teaspoon pepper

Additional basil sprigs

For the Balsamic Glaze, heat the vinegar in a saucepan over medium heat until reduced to $^3/_4$ cup.

For the Salad, cut the tomatoes and cheese into $^1/_4$-inch slices. Cut out any hard tomato cores. Wash and dry the basil.

For each serving, layer a slice of tomato, a slice of cheese and a basil leaf on a salad plate. Repeat the layers twice more.

Garnish with a basil sprig. Drizzle with 2 tablespoons of Balsamic Glaze.

Chill leftover Balsamic Glaze in the refrigerator. Remove from the refrigerator and allow to come to room temperature before serving.

The Heirloom Salad has become a favorite in the Pelican Club. While all the items that make up the salad are essential, the reason behind its popularity is the Balsamic Vinegar. In the PC, the chefs use an aged Aceto balsamic vinegar.

She was a woman in a man's kitchen but she was never intimidated. With an infectious smile, a totally disarming giggle, and cat-that-swallowed-the-canary grin, no one could resist Madie's charm. She was every employee's restaurant mother, and when her restaurant children hurt Madie cried. She was totally in her element on Saturday nights, and as the orders poured in you could hear her "echo" grow louder and louder as the shift wore on. When the pressure was on, however, she could work culinary miracles for rookies "in flames," especially when a new waitress whispering through tears explained that she had forgotten to order a stuffed flounder. Gone but not forgotten, we at Gaido's who shared Madie with the world remember how good she was at what she did, her laughter, and her tears, but most of all how much better we felt about ourselves when we were with her.

Raymond "Jabo" Smith, Madie Kimble, James Peques, and Paulie Gaido

Glazed Pear Salad

Makes 4 to 6 servings

Candied Pecans

4	egg whites
1	cup water
1/2	cup granulated sugar
1/2	teaspoon salt
1/2	teaspoon cinnamon
4	ounces pecan halves

Balsamic Vinaigrette

1/2	cup balsamic vinegar
1	teaspoon salt
1	teaspoon coarsely ground pepper
2	cups vegetable oil

Salad

4	tablespoons unsalted butter
2	teaspoons nutmeg
2	teaspoons cinnamon
4	tablespoons light brown sugar
4	Bosc pears, cored, sliced
4	tablespoons Grand Marnier
4	ounces red oak lettuce
1	head Boston Bibb lettuce
1	head frisée

Salt and pepper to taste

For the Candied Pecans, preheat the oven to 250 degrees. Beat the egg whites and water in a bowl until frothy. Combine the sugar, salt and cinnamon in a bowl.

Add the pecans to the egg white mixture and toss to coat. Remove pecans to the sugar mixture and toss to coat.

Arrange pecans evenly over a baking sheet lined with parchment paper. Bake for 15 minutes or until the sugar is crystallized; let cool.

For the Balsamic Vinaigrette, combine the vinegar, salt and pepper in a food processor and pulse until blended. Drizzle the oil in the processor to emulsify.

For the Salad, melt the butter in a large sauté pan over low heat. Add the nutmeg, cinnamon and brown sugar and mix well. Add the pears and cook until tender. Add the Grand Marnier and cook until the liquid is reduced to a syrup consistency; let cool.

Tear the red oak lettuce, bibb lettuce and frisée into 1-inch squares and place in a bowl. Toss with half the Vinaigrette. Season with salt and pepper. Divide the lettuce among serving plates. Sprinkle with the Candied Pecans.

Reheat the pears and the liquid, cooking until slightly thickened.

Arrange the pears in a fan over the salad. Drizzle with the remaining Balsamic Vinaigrette.

Au Gratin Potatoes

Makes 6 to 8 servings

3 pounds Idaho potatoes, peeled
2 cups milk
1 teaspoon garlic powder
1 tablespoon salt
1/2 tablespoon pepper
4 ounces Monterey Jack cheese, shredded
16 ounces Cheddar cheese, shredded

Cut the potatoes into 1/4-inch strips. Combine the potatoes and water to cover in a stockpot. Bring to a boil. Cook for 10 minutes; drain. Let cool to room temperature.

Combine the milk, garlic powder, salt and pepper in a bowl so the seasonings will be evenly distributed.

Combine the milk mixture, cheeses and potatoes in a large bowl or deep pan and mix well. Chill in the refrigerator for at least 2 hours.

Preheat the oven to 350 degrees. Remove the potatoes to individual ovenproof dishes. Bake for 20 to 30 minutes or until slightly brown on top.

The object with Gaido's Au Gratin Potatoes is to produce potatoes that are creamy and cheesy at the same time. It is important that the potatoes soak up milk overnight in the refrigerator. For a golden brown topping, we sprinkle extra cheese over the top. Don't be afraid to use extra-sharp Cheddar cheese if you want to intensify the cheese flavor, or to substitute heavy cream for the milk.

Brentwood Polenta, Mashed Sweet Potatoes, and Creamed Spinach

Mashed Sweet Potatoes

Makes 6 to 8 servings

2 pounds sweet potatoes,
  peeled, diced
Vegetable oil for coating
1/2 cup orange juice
2 tablespoons butter

2 tablespoons maple syrup
2 tablespoons Chicken Stock
  (page 73)
1 teaspoon salt

Preheat the oven to 400 degrees. Combine the sweet potatoes with a little oil in a bowl. Spread the sweet potatoes over a baking sheet.

Bake the sweet potatoes until fork-tender.

Simmer the orange juice in a large saucepan until it is reduced by half. Add the sweet potatoes, butter, syrup, Chicken Stock and salt. Cook for 10 minutes.

Mash the sweet potato mixture to the desired consistency.

Creamed Spinach

Makes 10 servings

1/2 pound bacon
1 cup diced yellow onions
Vegetable oil for sautéing
1 1/2 pounds fresh spinach, washed
2 roasted garlic cloves
4 ounces canned artichoke hearts

1 1/2 cups heavy cream
1 tablespoon salt
1 teaspoon pepper
6 ounces cream cheese
4 ounces fontina cheese, cubed
2 ounces Cheddar cheese, cubed

Fry the bacon until the fat is rendered. Drain the fat. Chop the bacon and set aside.

Sauté the onions in a little oil in a sauté pan until translucent.

Add the spinach and garlic; cook until the spinach is wilted and the liquid has evaporated.

Add the artichokes and cook for 3 to 5 minutes. Add the cream, salt, pepper, cheeses and bacon. Cook for 15 minutes, stirring frequently.

Brentwood Polenta

Makes 6 to 8 servings

3   garlic cloves, minced
2   shallots, minced
1/2   cup corn
Vegetable oil for sautéing
2   cups Chicken Stock (page 73)
3/4   cup cornmeal
1   cup heavy cream
2   ounces Grana Padana cheese, grated
1   tablespoon sugar
1/2   teaspoon salt
1/4   teaspoon pepper

Sauté the garlic, shallots and corn in a little vegetable oil in a sauté pan for 2 to 3 minutes. Add the Chicken Stock and bring to a boil.

Reduce the heat and whisk in the cornmeal. Cook for 5 minutes.

Add the cream, cheese, sugar, salt and pepper and mix well.

Gorgonzola Grits

Makes 4 to 6 servings

1   cup quick-cooking grits
2   cups Chicken Stock (page 73)
2   cups heavy cream
3/4   cup Gorgonzola cheese, crumbled
2   tablespoons sour cream
1   teaspoon salt

Combine the grits, Chicken Stock and cream in a saucepan. Cook over medium heat for 10 minutes until thickened and well-blended.

Remove from the heat. Stir in the cheese, sour cream and salt; mix well.

Truffled Mac & Cheese

Makes 4 to 6 servings

3 tablespoons salt
5 ounces elbow macaroni
2 cups heavy cream
2 teaspoons salt
4 tablespoons black truffle oil
16 ounces white Cheddar cheese, shredded
4 ounces Fontina cheese, shredded
3 tablespoons flour
1/4 teaspoon white pepper
1 recipe Baked Topping (page 113)

Bring 4 to 6 cups of water and 2 tablespoons salt to a boil in a medium stockpot. Add the macaroni and cook until al dente; drain.

Heat the cream, 2 teaspoons salt and the truffle oil in a saucepan over low heat. Add the cheeses and cook until melted, stirring.

Add the flour and cook until thick, stirring. Remove from the heat.

Add the cheese mixture and pepper to the macaroni; mix well.

Preheat the oven to 375 degrees. Spoon the macaroni into a baking dish.

Cover with a layer of Baked Topping.

Bake for 10 minutes, or until slightly brown on top.

Gaido's has been blessed for twenty-five years having
Estelcio Chevez as their truly gifted fish cutter.

Entrées

"It is no coincidence that the foods enjoyed most are those

native to the region in which they are served."

Entrées

Seafood Entrées

Soft-Shell Fritz

Crab au Gratin

Tiger Shrimp

Fried Shrimp

Stuffed Shrimp

CY's Demise

Deluxe Oysters

Oysters Brochette

Stuffed Flounder

Brentwood Halibut

Pecan-Encrusted Redfish

Grilled Salmon Nick

Baked Sea Bass

Snapper Fra Diavolo

Castilla Tuna

Non-Seafood Entrées

Cast-Iron Steaks

Veal Marsala

Pork Chops Sapporito

Chambord Duck

Chicken Rasmussen

Elements of Gulf Cuisine
LOCAL INGREDIENTS

It is no coincidence that the foods enjoyed most are those *native* to the region in which they are served: the smoothest Calvados are found in Normandy, the juiciest lobster clubs remain in Boston, and the most tender beef brisket exists in those countless smokehouses scattered throughout Texas. This ultimately explains why the two most popular fish on Gaido's menu are also the most common native fish. Red snapper and Gulf flounder have been staples on Gaido's menu for many years, though popularity and great demand have made them increasingly hard to obtain. In Texas, there is no law mandating that an establishment sell exactly what the menu states, so many restaurants and seafood purveyors pass off grouper, drum, or tilapia as red snapper or flounder. Studying up on the characteristics of each when purchasing them will help ensure you are getting exactly what you want.

Many of the living things that inhabit the ocean are "painted" by Mother Nature, often using her most vibrant colors. Regardless of the color, extremely fresh seafood will reflect artificial light, even in a display case. Within days of being removed from the water, fresh seafood's naturally vivid colors begin to fade and its reflection of light is lost.

Fresh seafood has the texture of and "feel" of a living organism and generally feels firm to the touch with more "bounce-back" when pressed with a fingertip. If you press down with your fingertip and feel that with little effort you could leave a noticeable impression, your sense of touch is telling you to seek out another option. Your sense of smell is also a guide—quality seafood does not smell fishy. In fact, the very freshest seafood has very little if any odor other than the smell of the sea.

Elements of Gulf Cuisine

CRAB

Gaido's Seafood Restaurant buys and sells more than ten thousand pounds of crab each year. More than 95 percent of all the crab purchased comes from Texas and Louisiana waters. Crab meat from Texas and Louisiana is of the best quality when purchased from May through October. While crab meat is available virtually year-round, the quality suffers as the water temperature decreases. Texas and Louisiana crab meat purchased during the winter months tends to be significantly inferior in quality. Crab meat from Mexico, on the other hand, is often excellent all year-round thanks to the country's temperate climate.

Once picked, crab meat can maintain its quality for seven days or longer if stored under proper refrigeration. When shopping for fresh crab meat, examine the container and the crab's origin. Ask whether the state where the crab meat was processed requires the process date to be printed on the container.

Soft Shells

As they grow, crabs molt and shed their exoskeletons. Soft-shell crabs are harvested as quickly as possible after they have shed their hard-shell covering. Most American soft-shell crabs are produced in the Chesapeake Bay area and are flash frozen as soon as possible after being harvested. When properly handled, carefully thawed, and

cooked immediately thereafter, frozen soft-shell crabs can yield excellent quality.

Soft-Shell Fritz

Egg Wash

3   eggs
1/2   cup milk

Wade Seasoning

1   to 1 1/4 cups all-purpose flour
1   teaspoon salt
1   teaspoon minced garlic
1/2   teaspoon pepper
1   teaspoon onion powder

Fritz Topping

3   ounces jumbo lump crab meat
1   teaspoon diced poblano pepper
1   teaspoon diced red bell pepper
Seasoned salt to taste

Soft-Shell Crabs

2   soft-shell crabs
12   tablespoons butter
6   tablespoons San Jacinto Butter (page 111)

For the Egg Wash, combine the eggs and milk in a bowl; mix well.

For the Wade Seasoning, combine the flour, salt, garlic, pepper and onion powder in a bowl; mix well.

For the Fritz Topping, combine the crab meat, poblano pepper, bell pepper and seasoned salt in a bowl; mix gently to avoid breaking crab lumps.

For the Soft-Shell Crabs, dip the crabs into the Egg Wash, then the Wade Seasoning. Repeat two more times.

Melt the butter in a sauté pan and pan-fry the crabs. (Or deep-fry them in oil, if preferred.)

Melt the San Jacinto butter in a sauté pan. Add the Fritz Topping and sauté until peppers are tender.

Spread the crabs with Fritz Topping.

Crab au Gratin

Makes 5 servings

Au Gratin Sauce

2	cups half-and-half
2	teaspoons Worcestershire sauce
2	tablespoons butter
2	tablespoons all-purpose flour
1	tablespoon dry sherry
1/2	teaspoon lemon juice
1/2	teaspoon Old Bay seasoning
3/4	cup shredded Monterey Jack cheese
1/3	teaspoon sugar

Assembly

1 1/4	pounds lump crab meat
2 1/2	cups shredded Cheddar-Jack cheese
5	ounces Baked Topping (page 113)

For the Au Gratin Sauce, heat the half-and-half and Worcestershire sauce in a saucepan.

Melt the butter in a saucepan. Stir in the flour; cook for 10 minutes or until the flour begins to brown and the mixture forms a roux, stirring constantly to prevent burning and lumps.

Stir the roux into the half-and-half mixture. Add the sherry, lemon juice, Old Bay seasoning, cheese and sugar; mix well. Remove from the heat.

For the Assembly, preheat the oven to 400 degrees. Line au gratin pans with crab meat. Top with Au Gratin Sauce, smoothing the top. Sprinkle with the cheese. Top with Baked Topping. Bake until bubbling.

Tiger Shrimp

Makes 2 servings

1 cup Crab Cake Mixture (page 55)
$^1/_2$ cup bread crumbs
1$^1/_2$ tablespoons Gaido's Mayonnaise (page 70)
1$^1/_2$ ounces bacon, cooked, crumbled
$^1/_2$ jalapeño pepper, roasted, chopped
8 shrimp, peeled, deveined, butterflied
Balsamic Glaze (page 88)

Combine the Crab Cake Mixture with the bread crumbs, mayonnaise, bacon and jalapeño in a bowl; mix well.

Preheat the oven to 400 degrees. Divide stuffing into 6 portions. Stuff into shrimp. Arrange the shrimp on a greased baking pan.

Roast for 10 to 12 minutes until the stuffing is hot and the shrimp are pink and firm.

Drizzle with Balsamic Glaze in a crisscross pattern to achieve "tiger stripes."

Fried Shrimp

Seasoned Cracker Meal

1/2	pound cracker meal
1	teaspoon salt
1	teaspoon garlic powder
1	teaspoon onion powder
1/2	teaspoon white pepper

Shrimp

2	eggs
1/2	cup milk
8	jumbo shrimp, peeled, tails left on, deveined
2	quarts vegetable oil

For the Seasoned Cracker Meal, stir together the cracker meal, salt, garlic powder, onion powder and white pepper in a bowl. Spread the mixture over a large rimmed sheet pan.

For the Shrimp, combine the eggs and milk in a large bowl and mix well.

Dip shrimp in the egg mixture and allow the excess to drip back into the bowl for 10 seconds.

Coat each shrimp evenly, save for the tail, with the Seasoned Cracker Meal.

Lay each shrimp with the deveined side down and press firmly with the heel of your palm to flatten.

Heat the oil in a stockpot to 350 degrees

Cook the shrimp in the oil for 2 to 3 minutes or until coating is golden brown; drain.

Stuffed Shrimp

Makes 2 servings

Seafood Stuffing

1	cup chopped yellow onion

Vegetable oil

1	tablespoon chopped celery
6	tablespoons melted butter
2¹/₂	teaspoons seasoned salt
6	drops hot pepper sauce
¹/₂	tablespoon Worcestershire sauce

Pinch of cayenne pepper

³/₄	cup fresh bread cubes

Shrimp

12	jumbo shrimp, peeled, deveined
6	eggs
³/₄	cup milk

All-purpose flour for coating

10	ounces Seasoned Cracker Meal (page 106)
6	cups canola oil

For the Seafood Stuffing, sweat the onion in a little oil in a sauté pan until translucent; drain any liquid.

Add the celery to the pan. Submerge the pan in ice water to cool.

Combine onion, celery, butter, seasoned salt, pepper sauce, Worcestershire sauce and cayenne pepper in a bowl; mix well. Add the bread cubes and mix well.

Form 2-tablespoon portions of the bread mixture into cylinders.

For the Shrimp, wrap a shrimp around a stuffing portion, pressing the shrimp firmly around the stuffing.

Combine the eggs and milk in a bowl; mix well.

Roll the shrimp in flour, then dip into egg mixture. Allow excess to drip back into the bowl. Roll the shrimp in the Seasoned Cracker Meal.

Heat the canola oil in a stockpot to 350 degrees.

Fry the shrimp in the oil for up to 1 minute until golden brown.

If ever there was a restaurant patron saint for "swamped" waiters and the parents of cranky babies it was Miss Liz. She was respected and admired by every employee because she coupled unwavering professionalism with warmth and consideration for others, especially servers "in the weeds." She was every inch a lady in language, style, and demeanor and a sight to behold when arriving in her church best on Sunday mornings. Her winning smile, gracious manner, and irresistible charm endeared her to generations of Pelican Club members. Parents dining with their small children were frequently surprised and always sublimely grateful when Miss Liz deftly kidnapped cranky little ones from their high chairs and booster seats for a tour of the dining room and kitchen.

Tradewinds bartender, Gaido's sommelier, and eventual maître d'hôtel, Jesse Castilla made all the stops on the way to becoming the very first Pelican Club manager, and the experience served him well. Confident and polished, he had a phenomenal memory for names. There was absolutely nothing that transpired in any dining room that surprised or flustered him, and his unflappable demeanor, especially in stressful situations, calmed the staff and comforted the guests. Jesse and Elizabeth Rhyne were the welcoming and familiar faces of the Pelican Club in its early years and helped set the Club's standard for professional yet personal service.

Elizabeth Rhyne

Elements of Gulf Cuisine
OYSTERS

Less than five miles from the back door of Gaido's restaurant is one of the world's largest oyster estuaries. Famous for the type and quantity of oysters, Galveston Bay produces on average over three million pounds of oysters each year during harvest season. Texas and Louisiana oysters are of the best quality when purchased from November through April. Harvesting is usually allowed only in the colder months of the year; this is to ensure full, plump oysters as opposed to the thin, watery oysters that are common when harvested in the summer months.

While it is difficult to determine the quality of an unshucked oyster, opening one out of a bag or box will be a good indicator for what the others will look like. An oyster that fills its shell to the edges is ideal. Occasionally oysters will have a red tint to them; this is due to the red algae and high oxygen levels in the water in which they were harvested, but this is completely harmless. If desired, place the oysters in a container of cold clean water to allow the natural filters to excrete the red tint and return to their normal color.

Oysters can be frozen, but there is a serious diminution in quality. When shopping for oysters, ask whether the state where the oysters were harvested requires the date of harvest to be printed on the container. The best option when purchasing oysters is to do so from someone who has earned your trust.

CY's Demise and Gorgonzola Grits

CY's Demise

Makes 1 dozen oysters

San Jacinto Butter

2 tablespoons minced garlic

1 tablespoon minced yellow onion

4 tablespoons white wine

16 tablespoons butter

4 tablespoons fresh lemon juice

1 teaspoon salt

$1/2$ teaspoon pepper

Oysters

12 oysters on the half shell

4 ounces grated Parmesan cheese

2 tablespoons finely chopped fresh parsley

For the San Jacinto Butter, sauté the garlic and onion in the white wine in a sauté pan until very tender. Combine the garlic, onions, wine, butter, lemon juice, salt and pepper in a blender; process to purée.

For the Oysters, melt the San Jacinto Butter in a small saucepan. Brush the oysters generously with the San Jacinto Butter until coated all over. Sprinkle the cheese over the oysters.

Grill the oysters for 5 to 10 minutes until the butter bubbles. Watch closely to ensure cheese doesn't burn. Sprinkle with chopped parsley.

Deluxe Oysters

Makes 1 dozen

12   oysters, on the half shell

Preheat the oven to 350 degrees. Arrange the oysters on a baking sheet.

Top two oysters with 2 tablespoons each of the 6 toppings (following). Bake for 15 to 20 minutes or until the toppings are golden brown and bubbly.

—

Each topping recipe yields approximately 1 quart

Rockefeller Topping
2   bunches green onions, sliced
Vegetable oil
12   tablespoons salted butter
9   tablespoons shredded
     Parmesan cheese
1   pound fresh spinach
4   tablespoons Worcestershire
     sauce
1/2 teaspoon Tabasco sauce
1/2 tablespoon minced garlic
3   anchovies
1   tablespoon minced
     jalapeño pepper
1   teaspoon Pernod

For the Rockefeller Topping, sweat the green onions in a little vegetable oil in a sauté pan until they release their liquid. Cook until translucent. Add the butter. Purée the onions and butter in a blender. Add the Parmesan cheese; mix well.

Cook the spinach in a sauté pan until most of the moisture cooks out. Combine the Worcestershire sauce, Tabasco sauce, garlic, anchovies, jalapeño and Pernod in a food processor; process until smooth. Combine with the green onion mixture; mix very well.

—

Bienville Topping

1 cup chopped yellow onion

Vegetable oil

1/4 cup butter

1 teaspoon paprika

1/2 teaspoon salt

1 teaspoon white pepper

1 teaspoon Louisiana hot sauce

1/4 cup white wine

1/4 teaspoon cayenne pepper

1 teaspoon lobster base (optional)

1 cup heavy cream

6 tablespoons grated Parmesan cheese

3/4 cup chopped mushrooms

1 cup shrimp, peeled, deveined

1 cup bread crumbs

2 egg yolks

For the Bienville Topping, sweat the onions in a little oil in a sauté pan until they release their liquid. Cook until caramelized. Add the butter, paprika, salt, white pepper, hot sauce, wine and cayenne pepper. Bring to a boil.

Add the lobster base; mix well. Add the cream; return to a boil. Turn off the burner. Add the Parmesan cheese; mix well. Add the mushrooms, shrimp, bread crumbs and egg yolks; mix well.

Baked Topping

6 ounces crushed saltine crackers

1 1/2 teaspoons garlic powder

1/2 teaspoon pepper

10 tablespoons butter, softened

For the Baked Topping, grind the crackers to fine crumbs in a food processor.

Add the garlic powder, pepper and butter; mix well.

Recipe continued on page 114

Ponzini Topping

1/2 pound yellow onions, chopped
Vegetable oil
1 tablespoon chicken base
3/4 pound mushrooms
1 cup heavy cream
1/4 cup white wine
1/2 teaspoon cayenne pepper
1/4 teaspoon salt
1/8 teaspoon nutmeg
2 1/2 egg yolks
2 1/2 cups shredded Swiss cheese
1 1/2 cups grated Parmesan cheese

For the Ponzini Topping, sweat the onions in a little oil in a sauté pan until they release their liquid. Cook until browned. Combine with the chicken base, mushrooms, cream, wine, cayenne pepper, salt and nutmeg in a stockpot. Bring to a simmer; reduce the heat to low. Add the Swiss cheese and cook until melted, stirring constantly. Add the Parmesan cheese and cook until melted, stirring constantly.

Stir a little of the hot liquid into the egg yolks to temper them. Add a little more liquid; mix well. Add the egg yolks to the sauce; mix well. Cook over low heat for 20 to 30 minutes.

Monterey Topping

2 cups half-and-half
1 tablespoon Worcestershire sauce
2 tablespoons butter
2 tablespoons all-purpose flour
1 tablespoon dry sherry
1/2 teaspoon lemon juice
1/2 teaspoon Old Bay seasoning
1/3 teaspoon sugar
1 cup shredded Monterey Jack cheese

For the Monterey Topping, heat the half-and-half and Worcestershire sauce in a saucepan.

Melt the butter in a saucepan. Stir in the flour; cook for 10 minutes or until the flour begins to brown and the mixture forms a roux, stirring constantly to prevent burning and lumps. Stir the roux into the half-and-half mixture.

Add the sherry, lemon juice, Old Bay seasoning, sugar and cheese; mix well. Remove from the heat.

NOTE: *For the sixth topping refer to recipe for Asiago Sauce on page 68.*

Oysters Brochette

Makes 12 brochettes

6 thick slices bacon
12 large oysters, shucked
$^1/_2$ cup Wade Seasoning (page 103)
4 tablespoons vegetable oil
$^1/_2$ cup diced yellow onion

Cut each bacon slice into halves. Wrap a bacon slice around an oyster and thread onto a long skewer. Repeat with remaining bacon and oysters, threading all onto one skewer.

Spread the Wade Seasoning on a work surface. Roll the bacon-wrapped oysters in the seasoning to coat thickly and evenly.

Heat the oil in a cast-iron skillet over medium heat. Add the skewer and cook for 3 to 4 minutes until deeply browned. Turn and cook the other side for 2 to 3 minutes.

Add the onions to the pan and cook for 1 minute. Serve the skewers on a bed of onions.

Oysters just love bacon, and the object for creating Oysters Brochette is to produce oysters that are both crisp and full of bacon flavor. The best way to achieve this is to fry bacon and save the drippings. When you bread the oysters make sure to gently pat them with your hand so they flatten out, which will maximize the contact surface with the frying pan. You don't need more than about $^1/_4$ inch of bacon drippings in the pan. Be sure to cook the oysters until they are brown and crisp. Most restaurants, some who are quite famous, deep-fry their oysters brochette. Once having tasted our recipe we believe you'll see the difference.

Stuffed Flounder

Makes 2 servings

1 (1½-pound) whole flounder
6 tablespoons San Jacinto Butter, melted (page 111)
8 to 12 ounces Seafood Stuffing (page 107)

Cut the flounder with a very sharp knife down to the bone along both sides of the spine from 1 inch behind the head to 1 inch from the tail. Make a perpendicular cut 3 to 4 inches long at each end of the lengthwise cuts.

Cut the fish from the bones on both sides of the spine, beginning at the head and working toward the tail, pulling to loosen the meat. Cut to within ½ inch of the lateral border of the fish. Press down on the knife to cut through the bones, but don't cut through the bottom of the fish. Repeat on the other side of the spine. Hold the fish with one hand and slide your other hand under the bones at the head of the fish. Pull firmly but gradually to remove the bones.

Preheat the oven to 350 degrees. Heat a rimmed baking sheet or glass baking dish in the oven; brush with a little of the San Jacinto Butter.

Brush the Butter over the fish. Spread the Stuffing mixture in the cavity. Fold to enclose the Stuffing. Brush with the Butter.

Pour ¼ cup water into the bottom of the baking sheet. Arrange the fish on the sheet. Bake for 15 to 20 minutes. Fish is ready when the thickest part is still very slightly transparent. Remove from the oven; fish will continue to cook.

No one living can remember when stuffed flounder was first offered on Gaido's menu, but it is likely to have been served for at least sixty years. Just as cooking turkey dressing in the body of the bird imparts moistness and important flavor components, the single step of slowly cooking the Seafood Stuffing in the flounder achieves the same effect. The best flounder for stuffing are from a pound-and-a-half to two pounds, although smaller and larger flounders can certainly be stuffed successfully as well.

Brentwood Halibut

Makes 4 servings

Mango Salsa

1	cup diced mango
1/2	cup diced yellow onion
1	cup diced red bell pepper
2	cups diced tomato
4	tablespoons chopped cilantro
2	tablespoons lime juice
1	teaspoon salt
1	teaspoon pepper

Halibut and Assembly

4	eggs
1	cup milk
1 3/4	cups crushed cornflakes
4	(6-ounce) halibut fillets
8	tablespoons butter
6	ounces Brentwood Polenta (page 96)

For the Mango Salsa, combine all ingredients in a bowl; mix well. Chill in the refrigerator.

For the halibut, combine the eggs and milk in a bowl; mix well. Spread the cornflake crumbs over a work surface.

Dip the Halibut into the egg mixture, then coat with the crumbs.

Sauté the halibut in the butter in a sauté pan over medium heat for 2 minutes on each side.

Remove the halibut from the pan. Let stand 30 seconds. Top with 1/3 to 1/2 cup salsa. Serve over Brentwood Polenta.

Pecan-Encrusted Redfish

Makes 5 servings

Slurry

2	tablespoons cornstarch
3	tablespoons white wine

Corn Relish

4	ears corn
2	poblano peppers, diced
2	red bell peppers, diced
1	red onion, diced
5	tablespoons sugar
2	teaspoons salt
1	teaspoon pepper
2$^{1}/_{2}$	cups cream

Pecan Crust

2	cups pecans, ground
2	cups panko
$^{1}/_{2}$	cup all-purpose flour
2	tablespoons salt
1	tablespoon pepper

Fish and Assembly

5	eggs
3	tablespoons water
7	to 10 redfish fillets

Butter for sautéing

For the Slurry, combine the cornstarch and wine in a bowl and stir to form a paste.

For the Corn Relish, remove the husks from the corn. Roast the corn over open flames; let cool.

Cut the kernels from the cobs. Combine the corn, peppers, onion, sugar, salt, pepper and cream in a large saucepan. Bring to a boil. Add the slurry and reduce the heat; simmer for 10 minutes.

For the Pecan Crust, combine the ground pecans, panko, flour, salt and pepper in a bowl. Spread over a work surface.

For the Assembly, combine the eggs and water in a bowl; mix well. Dip the fish into the egg mixture. Coat with Pecan Crust.

Sauté the fish in butter in a large sauté pan for 5 to 6 minutes on each side until firm and opaque.

Serve each fillet with $^{1}/_{3}$ cup Corn Relish. Store the remaining Corn Relish in an airtight container in the refrigerator for up to 2 weeks.

Grilled Salmon Nick

Makes 1 serving

Salmon

1   (6-ounce) skinless salmon fillet
2   ounces melted butter
1   ounce Charcoal Seasoning
    (page 72)

Nick Topping

4   tablespoons San Jacinto Butter
    (page 111)
2   tablespoons heavy cream
1   avocado, chopped

1   teaspoon cilantro
1   teaspoon fresh lime juice
1/2 teaspoon cumin
2   tablespoons roasted red pepper,
    cut julienne
2   tablespoons poblano pepper,
    coarsely chopped
1/2 teaspoon salt
3   ounces (31- to 35-count) shrimp,
    peeled, deveined, boiled

For the Salmon, prepare a fire in a grill or preheat a gas grill. Brush the better-looking side of the salmon with melted butter. Season with the Charcoal Seasoning.

Place buttered side down on the grill; grill for 2 minutes. Brush the top with melted butter. Turn and cook for 1 minute longer until flesh is not quite cooked through. Remove from the heat; fish will continue to cook.

For the Nick Topping, melt the San Jacinto Butter with the cream in a sauté pan. Cook until reduced by half. Add the remaining ingredients; mix well.

Spoon the topping mixture over the salmon.

Baked Sea Bass

Makes 1 serving

1 (6-ounce) Chilean sea bass fillet
Vegetable oil for coating
1 tablespoon chopped fresh chervil
4 tablespoons olive oil
$^1/_6$ of a red onion, chopped
1 garlic clove, minced
3 mussels in the shell
3 clams in the shell
3 jumbo shrimp, peeled and deveined
4 tablespoons white wine
Salt and pepper to taste
4 tablespoons unsalted butter, divided

———

Coat the sea bass with vegetable oil. Sprinkle with the chervil.

Heat the olive oil in a sauté pan and add the red onion and garlic. Turn heat to high and add mussels, clams and shrimp. Add the wine and mix well. Turn the heat to low. Season with salt and pepper. Remove from the heat.

Preheat the oven to 375 degrees. Rub a sheet of parchment paper with 2 tablespoons of the butter.

Arrange the fish and sautéed seafood mixture in the center of the paper.

Dot the fish and seafood with the remaining 2 tablespoons butter. Fold the parchment to enclose the fish and seal it.

Bake on a baking sheet for 20 minutes. Serve immediately.

Snapper Fra Diavolo

Makes 4 servings

Fra Diavolo Sauce

4 tablespoons olive oil
12 thin rings red onion
12 garlic cloves, smashed
6 Roma tomatoes, seeded, cut into $1/4$-inch slices
$1 1/4$ teaspoons red pepper flakes
1 cup dry white wine
$3/4$ cup tomato juice
$3/4$ cup heavy cream
8 ounces (about 1 cup) fresh basil, cut into strips
8 ounces tiny shrimp
Salt and pepper to taste

Breading Mixture

$1/4$ cup all-purpose flour
2 tablespoons cornmeal
$1/3$ cup Parmesan cheese
4 teaspoons garlic powder
$3/4$ teaspoon onion powder
$3/4$ teaspoon pepper
1 teaspoon cayenne pepper

Snapper and Assembly

4 snapper fillets
$1/2$ cup butter

For the Fra Diavolo Sauce, heat the oil in a sauté pan and add the onion and garlic. Turn the heat to high and add the tomatoes. Cook for a few seconds and add the pepper flakes and white wine. Reduce the heat to simmer. Cook until the liquid is nearly evaporated.

Add the tomato juice and cream. Simmer until the liquid is reduced by half. Add the basil and shrimp. Simmer until the shrimp are thoroughly heated. Season with salt and pepper.

For the Breading Mixture, combine all the breading ingredients and mix well.

For the Assembly, pat the Breading Mixture onto the fish. Melt the butter in a sauté pan over medium-high heat and heat until hot. Add the fish and cook until golden brown on both sides.

Serve the fish topped with Fra Diavolo Sauce.

Castilla Tuna

Makes 4 servings

Blackening Seasoning

4	ounces paprika
6	ounces seasoned salt
4	ounces onion powder
4	ounces marjoram
4	ounces oregano
2	ounces thyme
6	ounces garlic powder
4	ounces cayenne pepper
2	ounces rosemary

Tuna and Assembly

4	(6-ounce) tuna steaks
8	tablespoons unsalted butter
8	tablespoons heavy cream
8	ounces Asiago Sauce (page 68)
1	cup crawfish tails

For the Blackening Seasoning, combine all the ingredients in a bowl. Pour into a shaker.

For the Tuna, preheat the oven to 300 degrees. Sprinkle 1/4 cup seasoning over both sides of each tuna steak.

Heat the butter in a cast-iron skillet over medium heat until it begins to bubble. Add the tuna. Sear on each side, taking care not to burn the seasoning.

Place the skillet in the oven. Cook to desired doneness.

Heat the cream in a saucepan and add the Asiago Topping and crawfish. Cook for 1 minute or until crawfish is thoroughly heated, stirring to blend.

Serve fish topped with crawfish mixture.

With meticulous detail, Jose Aceituno has consistently produced Gaido's
homemade items for over twenty years.

Cast-Iron Steaks

Makes 1 large steak

1 (12- to 16-ounce) rib-eye steak
1 cup plus 2 pinches kosher salt, divided

Heat a skillet over high heat for 2 minutes. Reduce heat to medium.

Pour 1 cup of the salt into the skillet. Spread with a dry cloth to cover the pan evenly. The pan is ready when a paper towel wiped over the pan surface comes away clean.

Pour out the salt. Pat the steak dry. Reheat the pan over medium-high heat.

Add the steak and top with a 5-pound weight. Cook for 1 minute. Remove the weight and sprinkle the steak with a pinch of the kosher salt.

Turn the steak and top with the weight. Cook for 1 minute. Remove the weight and sprinkle with a pinch of the kosher salt.

Continue turning, weighting and cooking to desired doneness. The steak should be a deep, dark brown outside.

The quality of a dish does not always come from its ingredients but sometimes rather its method of preparation. Creole influence placed large cast-iron pans in Gaido's kitchen in the 1950s, with some of those same pans being found in Gaido's kitchen to this day. With the recipe only calling for kosher salt, the importance of a properly cleaned and seasoned pan is the main factor in properly cooking this single elemental dish.

LEROY HARDEMAN

Leroy Hardeman was hired from the Jack Tar Hotel when it closed its doors and quickly found a new home in Gaido's sauté station. It wasn't long before his day-in-and-day-out performance and professionalism prompted a trial as kitchen manager to see if he also possessed the organization and leadership skills necessary to successfully crossover to the other side of the counter. He not only exceeded all expectations that first month but continued to do so for his entire career. In doing so, Leroy led as productive, consistent, and quality-oriented a kitchen as any in Gaido's long history, until chronic knee problems forced his premature retirement and ultimately contributed to his death. Leroy was disciplined, committed, resourceful, and very, very bright. The Gaido family is deeply grateful for his exemplary leadership and, while continuing to mourn the premature loss of so respected a kitchen manager, can't help but speculate that in a more enlightened age he might have made an excellent Texas governor or United States Senator.

Veal Marsala

Marsala Sauce

1	tablespoon olive oil
4	garlic cloves, minced
4	teaspoons minced shallots
4	tablespoons marsala, divided
2	cups shiitake mushrooms, sliced
1	cup heavy cream
1	teaspoon salt
1	teaspoon pepper
1/2	teaspoon fresh sage
1	tablespoon grated Parmesan cheese

2	tablespoons cornstarch
1	lemon, cut into halves

Veal Cutlets

2	veal cutlets

Salt and pepper to taste

1 1/2	cups all-purpose flour
2	eggs
4	tablespoons milk
4	tablespoons unsalted butter

For the Marsala Sauce, heat the olive oil in a sauté pan over medium to high heat. Add the garlic and shallots and cook until shallots are translucent.

Add 2 tablespoons of the marsala and heat to very hot. Ignite the marsala with a long match. Cook until the flames subside.

Add the mushrooms. Cook for 1 minute. Reduce the heat to low. Add the cream, salt, pepper, sage and Parmesan cheese and mix well.

Combine the remaining 2 tablespoons of marsala and the cornstarch in a small cup; mix well. Stir the mixture into the liquid in the sauté pan, whisking out any lumps. Bring to a boil.

Reduce the heat to low. Squeeze the lemon halves lightly and add the juice to the Marsala Sauce.

For the Veal Cutlets, sprinkle the veal with salt and pepper. Combine the flour with salt and pepper. Combine the eggs and milk in a bowl and mix well.

Dip the veal into the egg mixture. Coat with the flour.

Heat the butter in a large sauté pan over medium heat until butter begins to bubble.

Place the veal in the pan. Cook for 2 minutes on each side.

Serve the veal topped with Marsala Sauce.

Pork Chops Sapporito

Makes 2 servings

Sapporito Seasoning

2 cups crushed saltine crackers

1/8 cup garlic cloves, minced

1/4 cup dried oregano

1/4 cup garlic powder

3 teaspoons pepper

3 teaspoons salt

Pork Chops

4 eggs

1 cup milk

2 (8-ounce) double-bone pork chops, frenched

4 tablespoons unsalted butter

For the Sapporito Seasoning, combine the cracker crumbs and garlic in a food processor. Process until finely chopped.

Combine the crumb mixture, oregano, garlic powder, pepper and salt in a large bowl and mix well.

For the Pork Chops, preheat the oven to 300 degrees. Combine the eggs and milk in a bowl and mix well.

Dip the pork into the egg mixture, allowing the excess to drip back into the bowl.

Spread the Sapporito Seasoning over a work surface. Coat the pork with the seasoning, pressing it firmly onto all sides.

Heat the butter in a medium sauté pan until it begins to bubble.

Add the pork and sear on all sides.

Place the pan in the oven. Cook for 5 to 10 minutes or to desired doneness.

Chambord Duck

Duck

4   boneless duck breasts
Salt and freshly ground pepper to taste
1   tablespoon olive oil

Chambord Sauce

2   boxes blackberries
5   tablespoons Chambord, divided

———

For the Duck, sprinkle the duck with salt and pepper. Score the skin lightly with a sharp knife.

Pour the oil into a cold sauté pan. Arrange the duck in the pan skin side down. Turn heat to medium. Cook the duck until the skin is crisp and some of the fat has melted. Turn and cook the other side for about 6 minutes to medium-rare. Remove from the heat; let rest for 5 minutes. Reserve the drippings in the sauté pan.

For the Chambord Sauce, combine the blackberries and 4 tablespoons of the Chambord in a saucepan over medium heat. Cook for 20 minutes or until the berries break down and are very soft and the juice is thickened, stirring occasionally.

Press the mixture through a fine mesh strainer. Return the strained sauce to the saucepan. Add the remaining Chambord and 1 teaspoon duck drippings from sauté pan.

Cut the duck into thin slices. Drizzle with the Chambord Sauce.

Chicken Rasmussen

Makes 6 servings

Chicken

6 boneless chicken breasts, skinless or skin on

Flour

Salt and pepper to taste

Vegetable oil for frying

Rasmussen Sauce

1 1/2 tablespoons olive oil

1 tablespoon chopped garlic

3/4 cup sliced green onions

3 1/2 ounces sliced mushrooms

1/4 teaspoon red pepper flakes

1 tablespoon chopped chipotle pepper

3 cups heavy cream

4 tablespoons white wine

1 teaspoon cornstarch

14 ounces artichoke hearts, cut into quarters

1/4 cup capers

1/2 teaspoon thyme

1/4 cup grated Parmesan cheese

4 bacon slices, cooked and diced

1 tablespoon lemon juice

For the Chicken, preheat the oven to 350 degrees. Coat the chicken with flour, salt and pepper. Heat oil in a large sauté pan with an ovenproof handle. Add the chicken and cook until about half done.

Turn the chicken and cook for 2 minutes. Place the sauté pan in the oven. Bake for 10 minutes.

For the Rasmussen Sauce, heat the olive oil in a large sauté pan over medium heat. Sauté the garlic, green onions, mushrooms, pepper flakes and chipotle pepper until tender.

Add the cream. Cook until reduced by one-fourth.

Combine the wine and cornstarch in a small cup. Pour into the cream mixture. Add the artichoke hearts, capers, thyme, Parmesan cheese, bacon and lemon juice. Cook for 10 minutes until thickened.

Serve the chicken topped with Rasmussen Sauce.

The daily meetings that take place between managers and staff play a pivotal part in the intangible force that ensures the type of service expected from a centennial restaurant. An additional element unique to Gaido's is the waiters' classification through the color tie that they bear. Denoting their experience, ability, and tenure, the ties have stood the test of time.

Desserts

"Service should not be just part of their jobs,

but also part of their lives."

Desserts

Apple Butter Soufflé

Banana Bread Foster

Crème Brûlée

Cheesecake

Chocolate Mousse

S'Mores

Lemon Curd Tart

Pecan Pie

Key Lime Pie

Service

A GAIDO'S TRADITION

To be great at something one must understand that something in its entirety. Gaido's waiters know that *service* should not just be part of their jobs, but also part of their lives. Lasting relationships have been forged in this time-tested restaurant through day-to-day mentoring. Rather than hanging autographed photos of visiting celebrities, Gaido's honors those extended family members who have given their time and talent by adorning the rooms that bear their names with their portraits.

For over a century Gaido's has been blessed with an extraordinary service staff, perhaps best remembered in the forties, fifties, and sixties for their ability to accurately memorize customer orders simply by the power of concentration. Waiters like Raymond "Shades" Campbell, Clifton McCleland, Sam Houston, Clary Milburn, and Raymond "Jabo" Smith are all long gone but continue to set the standard for the thousands who follow their example and choose to put on a Gaido's uniform. Through the years the members of the most exceptional service staff have shared a critical skill set. First, they were able to show every single guest that they were grateful for the privilege of serving them. Second, they were thoroughly knowledgeable not only about Gaido's menu but about Gulf Coast seafood. Third, they acquired and honed their serving skills so they could flawlessly execute the fundamentals and add their own personal service touch. Fourth, they quickly and unobtrusively learned each of their guest's needs and preferences to tailor the Gaido's experience to meet and exceed the guest's expectations.

Apple Butter Soufflé

Makes 1 serving

Apple Cake

3 cups stale bread, cut into 1/2-inch cubes
2 cups finely chopped apples
1 cup walnuts, coarsely chopped
3 eggs
1 tablespoon cinnamon
1 teaspoon nutmeg
1/2 quart milk
1 cup heavy cream
2 cups granulated sugar
1 teaspoon vanilla extract
1/4 cup packed brown sugar
1/2 cup graham cracker crumbs

Apple Butter Sauce

1/4 cup Maker's Mark bourbon
1 cup heavy cream
1/2 cup packed brown sugar
1/4 cup apple butter
1/2 teaspoon salt

Apple Soufflé

1/2 cup egg whites
1 cup sugar
6 ounces prepared Apple Cake

For the Cake, preheat the oven to 350 degrees. Place the bread cubes on a sheet pan and toast until golden brown. The bread should have the texture of a crouton. Place the toasted bread cubes, apples and walnuts in a large mixing bowl and toss to combine.

Combine the eggs, cinnamon and nutmeg in a bowl and stir until the cinnamon and nutmeg dissolve. Add the milk, heavy cream, granulated sugar and vanilla to the egg mixture and stir until blended.

Pour the liquid mixture over the bread cubes and toss until the bread is coated. Let sit until the bread cubes are completely saturated.

Spoon the mixture into a large baking pan and top with the brown sugar and graham cracker crumbs. Bake for about 45 minutes. This cake makes 10 servings.

For the Apple Butter Sauce, set a medium sauté pan over high heat for 30 seconds. Pour in the bourbon. Ignite carefully with a long match. Turn off the heat. Let the alcohol burn off without reducing the bourbon further.

Add the cream, brown sugar, apple butter and salt to the pan. Whisk until well blended.

For the Apple Soufflé, preheat the oven to 350 degrees.

For many years dinner rolls were served at Gaido's along with Bama Apple Butter. This popular item often found its way to the dessert portion of the meal. Bama eventually discontinued the apple butter. In response to requests still heard today, this soufflé has been used to satisfy these longing palates, and it has started to make its way onto the dessert menu.

Whisk the egg whites in a bowl until frothy. Add the sugar gradually, beating until glossy peaks form a stiff meringue.

Break the cake into pieces in a large bowl. Add three-fourths of the meringue; mix gently.

Fill a large ramekin three-fourths full of the cake mixture. Use the remaining meringue to fill the ramekin to the top.

Bake the soufflé for 20 minutes.

Pour warm Apple Butter Sauce over the soufflé and serve immediately.

Banana Bread Foster

Banana Bread

1¼ cups unsalted butter, melted
2½ cups sugar
3   eggs, room temperature
1   teaspoon vanilla extract
3   to 4 overripe bananas, puréed
4   cups bread flour
2   teaspoons salt
2   teaspoons baking soda
2   cups coarsely chopped walnuts

Crème Anglaise

1   quart half-and-half
1   vanilla bean, split lengthwise
12   egg yolks
1¼ cups sugar

Brown Sugar Butter and Assembly

4   tablespoons unsalted butter
½   cup packed light brown sugar
4   tablespoons rum
Vanilla ice cream

For the Banana Bread, coat 3 loaf pans with nonstick cooking spray. Preheat the oven to 350 degrees.

Combine butter and sugar in a mixing bowl. Beat for a few minutes. Stir in the eggs, vanilla and bananas.

Add mixture of the flour, salt, baking soda and walnuts. Spoon the batter into the prepared pans. Set pans on a larger baking sheet. Bake for 45 minutes or until bread tests done. Turn the loaves out of the pans right away; let cool on a wire rack.

For the Crème Anglaise, bring the half-and-half and vanilla just to a boil in a heavy saucepan.

Beat the egg yolks and sugar in a mixing bowl. Add one-third of the hot mixture; mix well. Stir the egg mixture into the half-and-half mixture. Cook over medium heat, stirring constantly, until the sauce coats a spoon. Do not boil.

Strain through a fine strainer into a bowl. Chill over an ice bath. Cover and refrigerate for up to 4 days.

For the Brown Sugar Butter, burn off the alcohol from the rum in a saucepan over high heat. Reduce the heat when all the alcohol is burned off. Melt the butter in the saucepan over medium heat. Add the brown sugar; mix well.

Cut the Banana Bread into ½-inch slices. Cook in the Brown Sugar Butter until a caramelized coating forms. Turn and cook the other side.

Place the Banana Bread on a plate. Top with ice cream. Drizzle with Crème Anglaise.

KEWPIE GAIDO'S
CUT GLASS COLLECTION

"Kewpie" Gaido was born Maureen Schwerdtfeger. From the time she was a very small child she loved Kewpie dolls. It seemed to her father that she was never without one of the dolls under her arm, and it was from him that she received the nickname that she proudly carried all of her life. Her modest collection of Kewpies prompted her beloved Aunt Celeste to bequeath to Kewpie a collection of cut glass acquired over her lifetime, and it is Aunt Celeste's cut glass, enhanced with Kewpie's own acquisitions, that are displayed in both Gaido's Main Dining Room and Gulf Room.

Crème Brûlée

6 egg yolks
2 vanilla beans
5 cups heavy cream
1 cup sugar
$^{1}/_{2}$ teaspoon cinnamon
6 tablespoons turbinado sugar

Beat the egg yolks in a large bowl.

Split the vanilla beans lengthwise and scrape out the seeds. Combine the seeds with the cream, sugar and cinnamon in a saucepan. Bring to a boil; boil for 1 minute. Place the saucepan in ice water; cool to 120 degrees.

Preheat the oven to 300 degrees. Pour the cream mixture through a strainer into the egg yolks; mix well.

Divide the mixture among 8 ramekins. Arrange the ramekins in a shallow baking dish lined with a clean kitchen towel to prevent movement.

Add enough hot water to the baking dish to reach halfway up the sides of the ramekins.

Bake for 50 to 60 minutes. Remove the ramekins to the refrigerator. Chill for 8 hours or longer until set.

Sprinkle the turbinado sugar over each dessert. Use a kitchen torch to heat the sugar until it melts, then hardens.

Cheesecake

Makes 8 to 10 servings

Graham Cracker Crust
4 tablespoons sugar
9 whole graham crackers, crushed to crumbs
4 tablespoons butter

Cheesecake Filling
16 ounces cream cheese, softened
16 ounces sour cream
1 cup sugar
4 whole eggs

For the Graham Cracker Crust, preheat the oven to 325 degrees.

Combine the sugar and crumbs in a bowl; mix well. Melt the butter and add to the crumb mixture; mix well.

Spread the mixture over the bottom of a 9-inch springform pan. Press down to compact the crust. Bake for 5 minutes. Raise the oven temperature to 400 degrees.

For the Cheesecake Filling, beat the cream cheese in a large mixing bowl with a mixer on slow speed until it is the consistency of whipped cream, scraping the bowl frequently.

Add the sour cream; mix well. Add the sugar; mix well. Add the eggs one at a time, beating well after each addition. Pour the filling into the crust slowly.

Bake for 5 minutes. Turn the heat to 300 degrees. Bake for 60 to 70 minutes without opening the oven door. Let stand to cool at room temperature for 2 hours. Drizzle with your favorite topping.

TOM PONZINI

Recruited out of the Conrad Hilton School of Hotel and Restaurant Management, Tom Ponzini quickly became an indispensable part of Gaido's kitchen. Astonishingly focused and committed for someone so young, it was Tom who planned and inaugurated Gaido's In-House Bakery. In fact, all of the bread and many of the most famous dessert recipes are his own creations. Willing to spend a year abroad to further hone his culinary skills, Tom was selected as the outstanding student in his class at La Varenne in Paris. This is where he first conceived the recipe for Gaido's Shrimp Bisque, for which he is best known. With a long and prosperous career in food service firmly within his grasp, Tom chose to hear God's call and is now a deeply respected and much loved Roman Catholic priest. Though sorely missed in the kitchen, the Gaido family could not be prouder of Father Tom.

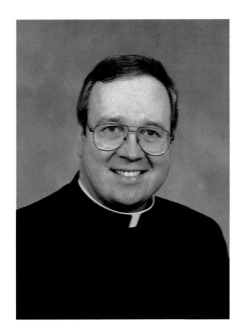

Chocolate Mousse

Makes 10 servings

8   ounces white chocolate
2 1/2   ounces semisweet
        chocolate chips
6   egg yolks
2   tablespoons unsalted
    butter, melted

1/2   cup heavy cream
2   tablespoons confectioners' sugar
8   eggs whites

Melt the white chocolate in a double boiler, stirring constantly. Remove from the heat and add the chocolate chips. Stir until the chips melt and the mixture is well blended; let cool.

Beat the egg yolks in a bowl set in an ice bath until thick and pale yellow. Add the butter in a slow, steady stream, beating constantly.

Add the chocolate mixture to the egg yolk mixture.

Beat the cream and sugar in a separate bowl set in an ice bath until medium-firm peaks form. Fold into the chocolate mixture.

Beat the egg whites with a mixer until stiff peaks form. Fold into the chocolate mixture and mix gently. Chill in the refrigerator.

Note: *If you are concerned about using raw eggs, use eggs pasteurized in their shells, which are sold at some specialty food stores.*

Chocolate mousse at its best is light, airy, delicate, and possesses an intense yet nuanced chocolate flavor. When made from scratch, the texture should have a grainy quality from the shreds of chocolate. Far from a pudding-like consistency or taste, Gaido's Chocolate Mousse is different than what most have come to expect from commercial mousses.

S'Mores

Makes 36 pieces

Graham Cracker Crust
2   cups graham cracker crumbs
4   tablespoons sugar
2/3   cup melted butter

Italian Meringue
2   cups sugar, divided
1/2   cup corn syrup or glucose
6   tablespoons water
8   egg whites, room temperature

Chocolate Ganache
1   pound bittersweet chocolate
1   pint heavy cream

Caramel Sauce
4 1/2   pounds sugar
2   cups water
4   tablespoons lemon juice
2   quarts heavy cream,
      at room temperature
10   tablespoons unsalted butter,
      cut into pieces

For the Graham Cracker Crust, preheat the oven to 350 degrees. Combine the crumbs and sugar in a bowl. Add the butter and mix with your hands. Press the mixture over the bottom of a 9×11-inch baking pan. Bake for 5 to 7 minutes. Cool completely. Chill in the refrigerator or freezer or cool at room temperature for 30 minutes.

For the Italian Meringue, combine 1 7/8 cups sugar with the corn syrup and water in a saucepan. Bring to a boil over high heat. Use a candy thermometer to monitor the temperature; when it reaches 220 degrees, put the egg whites into a mixing bowl and begin beating them.

Beat the egg whites until soft peaks form, then add the remaining 2 tablespoons of sugar. Remove the sugar syrup from the heat when it reaches 240 degrees. Pour a steady stream of hot syrup down the side of the bowl into the egg whites with the mixer set on high speed. Beat in all the syrup, then beat for 1 minute longer. Reduce the speed to medium; beat until the mixture is cool.

For the Chocolate Ganache, chop the chocolate into small pieces. Place in a metal bowl. Bring the cream to a boil; pour over the chocolate. Use a spatula to stir until the hot cream melts the chocolate; let cool to room temperature. (Ganache can be covered and chilled in the refrigerator for up to 1 month.)

For the Caramel Sauce, combine the sugar and water in a large saucepan. Stir to moisten the sugar. Bring the mixture to a boil over high heat, stirring constantly. Brush down the side of the pan with water and a pastry brush to remove any sugar crystals.

Add the lemon juice without stirring. Boil until the sugar turns a dark golden brown and has a rich aroma. Remove from the heat. Add the cream gradually, taking care as the caramel may splatter; mix well.

Add the butter pieces; mix well. Strain the sauce; let cool completely. (Caramel Sauce can be covered and chilled in the refrigerator for up to several weeks. Stir before using.)

For the S'mores, spread the Italian Meringue 1/2 inch thick over the crust. Place in the freezer to allow the meringue to set.

Heat 2 tablespoons of the Chocolate Ganache and 4 tablespoons of the Caramel Sauce in a saucepan; mix well.

Cut S'mores into 1×3-inch pieces. Toast 3 pieces under a broiler for 1 minute or with a kitchen torch until top is golden brown. Arrange on a dessert plate. Drizzle with warm Chocolate Ganache-Caramel Sauce or service it in a little dish on the side. Refrigerate any unused Ganache and Caramel Sauce as directed.

Lemon Curd Tart

Makes about 6 tarts

Sweet Tart Dough

12 tablespoons unsalted
   butter, softened
5 to 5$^{1}/_{2}$ cups confectioners' sugar
7 egg yolks
1 egg
3$^{1}/_{2}$ cups all-purpose flour
Flour for dusting

Lemon Curd

$^{1}/_{2}$ cup lemon juice
$^{3}/_{4}$ cup sugar, divided

2 teaspoons finely grated
  lemon zest
2 eggs
12 tablespoons butter, room
   temperature

Whipped Cream and Assembly

1 cup heavy cream
1 teaspoon vanilla extract
$^{1}/_{4}$ to $^{1}/_{2}$ cup confectioners'
  sugar, sifted
Strawberries

For the Sweet Tart Dough, beat the butter and confectioners' sugar in a mixing bowl. Whisk the egg yolks with the whole egg. Add to the butter mixture; mix well, scraping the side of the bowl as needed. Reduce mixer speed to low; add the flour. Mix just until incorporated. Dough should be firm and smooth, not sticky. Dust with flour. Wrap in plastic wrap. Chill in the refrigerator.

Preheat the oven to 350 degrees. Roll portions of the dough $^{1}/_{4}$ inch thick. Cut into 6-inch circles. Press the dough into tart molds. Bake until golden at the edges. Remove the crusts from the molds; let cool.

For the Lemon Curd, combine the lemon juice, 6 tablespoons of the sugar and the lemon zest in a nonreactive saucepan. Bring to a boil.

Whisk the eggs and remaining sugar in a nonreactive bowl just to combine. Pour one-fourth of the hot lemon juice mixture into the eggs; mix well. Add the eggs to the lemon juice in the pan. Bring to a boil, whisking constantly. Boil for 1 minute. Remove from the heat; chill in an ice bath until the mixture is 130 degrees.

Add the butter to the lemon mixture in five parts, mixing well after each addition. Use immediately, or cover and chill in the refrigerator.

For the Whipped Cream, combine the cream and vanilla in a stainless steel bowl. Beat with a whisk until cream begins to thicken. Add the confectioners' sugar. Whisk just until soft peaks form. Use immediately or cover and chill in the refrigerator for up to 4 days.

Spoon the Lemon Curd into the tart shells. Cut a strawberry into slices vertically. Arrange around the edge of the tarts, points facing inward. Fill the center with the remaining slices.

Spoon the Whipped Cream into a pastry bag fitted with a star tip. Pipe a rosette into the center of each tart. Serve immediately or refrigerate.

Pecan Pie

Makes 10 servings

Graham Cracker Crust

10	ounces graham cracker crumbs
1/4	cup sugar
3	tablespoons butter

Pecan Pie Filling

6	eggs
1 3/4	cups sugar
1/2	quart light corn syrup
1	tablespoon vanilla extract
1/2	teaspoon salt
1 1/4	cups pecans pieces, toasted

Cowboy Bourbon Sauce

1/4	cup water
1/4	cup sugar
1/4	cup bourbon
1/4	cup heavy cream
1	tablespoon vanilla extract

Assembly

6	tablespoons light corn syrup
2 1/2	cups pecan halves, toasted

For the Graham Cracker Crust, combine the crumbs and sugar in a bowl. Melt the butter and add to the crumb mixture; mix well.

Preheat the oven to 300 degrees. Line the outside of a springform pan with aluminum foil. Coat the pan with nonstick cooking spray. Press the crumb mixture over the bottom of the pan, using your palms to pack the mixture tightly and evenly to prevent the filling from leaking.

For the Pecan Pie Filling, combine the eggs, sugar, corn syrup, vanilla, salt and pecan pieces in a large bowl; mix well. Pour into the prepared crust. Bake for 1 hour or until the center is soft to the touch but edges are firm. Let cool for 15 minutes.

For the Cowboy Bourbon Sauce, bring the water and sugar to a boil in a saucepan to make a simple syrup. Add the bourbon, cream and vanilla and stir until fully incorporated.

For the Assembly, remove the warm pie from the springform pan. Invert on a cardboard round or cake platter. Let cool for 15 minutes longer.

Heat the corn syrup in a saucepan. Brush over the crust—bottom and side—of the pie with a pastry brush. Press the pecan halves into the syrup, pushing firmly. Brush Cowboy Bourbon Sauce over the pie while still warm.

This pecan pie, an original recipe of the Kewpie Schwerdtfeger Gaido Family, dates back to the early part of the last century. It was modified to become a "crustless" pie with a simple method: invert the pie after baking and the pecans become the crust. Add pecan halves to the top—VOILA!

Key Lime Pie

Makes 10 servings

Graham Cracker Crust

4	tablespoons sugar
9	whole graham crackers, crushed
4	tablespoons butter

Key Lime Filling

1/2	cup egg yolks
8	ounces cream cheese, softened
2 1/2	cups sweetened condensed milk
3/4	cup Key lime juice

Lime Mint Sauce

1	cup water
2	cups sugar
3	tablespoons lime juice
2	tablespoons fresh mint, chopped
1	tablespoon grated lime zest

For the Graham Cracker Crust, preheat the oven to 325 degrees.

Combine the sugar and crumbs in a bowl; mix well. Melt the butter and add to the crumb mixture; mix well.

Spread the mixture over the bottom of a 9-inch springform pan. Press down to compact the crust. Bake for 5 minutes; let cool. Reduce the oven temperature to 300 degrees.

For the Key Lime Filling, combine the egg yolks, cream cheese, condensed milk and Key lime juice in a blender; process until well blended. Pour into the crust. Bake for 15 minutes; let cool.

For the Lime Mint Sauce, combine the water, sugar, lime juice, mint and lime zest in a saucepan. Bring to a boil and cook until the sugar dissolves, stirring. Pour through a strainer and let stand to cool.

Serve the pie topped with Lime Mint Sauce.

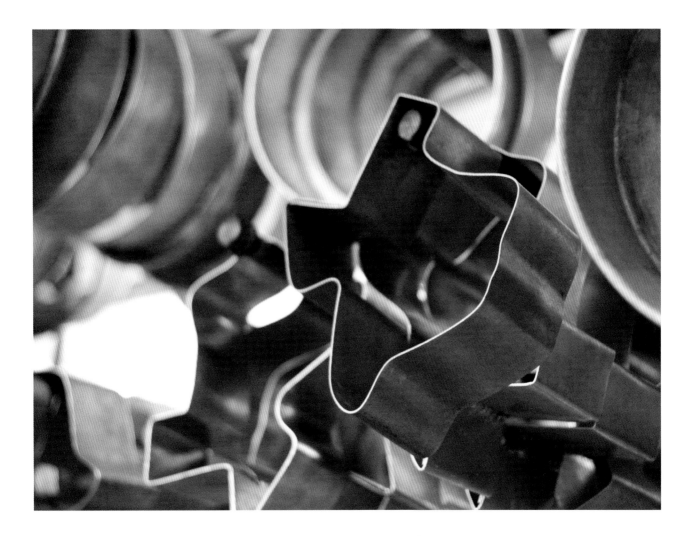

TEXAS PIE MOLD

Gaido's famous Pecan Pie has been a popular dessert request at the restaurant since its introduction to the menu. The pie continues to grow in popularity as a holiday gift to send to family and friends. Recently the delicious pie has taken on a new form, perfect for those who wish to send their loved ones a little "Taste of Texas."

Index

Gaido's

FAMOUS SEAFOOD RESTAURANT

A COOKBOOK CELEBRATING 100 YEARS

To order additional copies of our cookbook
and to order our homemade products, please visit our
Web site at www.gaidos.com.